LOVE'S PURE LIGHT

SPIRITUAL POEMS AND WRITINGS FOR THE SOUL

(INSPIRATION FOR THE SOUL)

WRITTEN FOR AND READ AT CATHOLIC
CHARASMATIC PRAYER GROUP MEETINGS
SPECIFICALLY FOR THE AWESOME AND POWERFUL
"CROWN OF GLORY PRAYER GROUP"

BY: ELIZABETH ANN MARKS

(INSPIRED BY THE HOLY SPIRIT)
(ALL GOOD THINGS COME FROM GOD)

Order this book online at www.trafford.com
or email orders@trafford.com

Most Trafford titles are also available at major online book retailers.

Printed in Victoria, BC, Canada.

ISBN: 978-1-4269-2822-2

*Our mission is to efficiently provide the world's finest, most comprehensive book publishing
service, enabling every author to experience success. To find out how to publish your book, your
way, and have it available worldwide, visit us online at www.trafford.com*

Trafford rev. 6/22/2010

 www.trafford.com

North America & international
toll-free: 1 888 232 4444 (USA & Canada)
phone: 250 383 6864 ♦ fax: 812 355 4082

ACKNOWLEDGEMENTS

FIRST OF ALL, I WANT TO THANK MY GOD FOR THE GIFT OF POETRY, AND FOR GIVING ME THE IMMENSE BLESSINGS, TO BE ABLE TO SPREAD HIS LOVING GRACE. I ALSO WANT TO THANK THE BELOVED LEADERS OF THE POWERFUL PRAYER GROUP, "THE CROWN OF GLORY, PRAYER GROUP". KEVIN ROY, WHO IS SO BLESSED BY GOD, AND HUMBLY LEADS THE GROUP IN WORSHIP AND PRAISE. THERESA ROY, KEVIN'S MOM, THE LITTLE WARRIOR, SO FILLED WITH THE HOLY SPIRIT, AND SHARES WITH US, THE LOVE OF GOD AND WHOM GOD WORKS THROUGH, TO SHOW HIS ALMIGHTY POWERS OF HEALING OF BODY, MIND AND SPIRIT TO ALL WHO BELIEVE. GEORGE ROY, KEVIN'S DAD WHO ALSO HAS A POWERFUL FAITH AND MANY GIFTS OF THE HOLY SPIRIT. I MYSELF, HAVE HAD MANY HEALINGS SINCE I HAVE BELONGED TO THIS GROUP. I HAVE ALSO WITNESSED AND HAVE HEARD WITNESS OF PEOPLE WHO HAVE RECEIVED AMAZING HEALINGS FROM GOD DUE TO THE PRAYERS OF HIS PRAYER WARRIORS AND HIS POWERFUL HOLY SPIRIT. TO ALL THE OTHERS, WHO DILIGENTLY PRAY FOR US FOR HEALING AND WHOLENESS, THERESA, GEORGE, KEVIN AND DEBBY ROY, DEBBY SAUNDERS, A GREAT LITTLE PRAYER WARRIOR, WHOSE FAITH IS AMAZING, DAVE, HELEN, RITA, AND SO MANY MORE THAT TAKE THEIR TIME TO PRAY FOR US IN THE PRAYER ROOMS. I WANT TO THANK BROTHER JACK, WHO ALSO SHARES HIS AMAZING FAITH WITH US. THIS FAITH OF HIS IS SO INSPIRING.

I WANT TO THANK ALL THE TEAM AT TRAFFORD PUBLISHING, WHO PATIENTLY GUIDED ME THROUGH MY FIRST BOOK. I HOPE THAT ALL WHO READ THIS BOOK ARE INSPIRED TO GO DEEPER IN THEIR FAITH AND ALL WHO DO NOT HAVE THIS DEEP FAITH, I HOPE THIS BOOK WILL INSPIRE THEM TO SEEK GOD MORE FULLY IN THEIR LIVES.
THANK YOU ALSO, MY BROTHERS AND SISTERS, IN CHRIST WHO ALSO ATTEND AND BELONG TO THIS WONDERFUL GROUP, FOR ENCOURAGING ME TO PUBLISH THESE POEMS WHICH THE LORD HAS SEEN FIT TO LET ME SHARE WITH THEM. I HOPE I HAVE NOT MISSED ANYONE WHO DESERVES MY THANKS FOR THEIR HELP AND ENCOURGAGEMENT. AGAIN, THANK YOU FROM THE BOTTOM OF MY HEART.

ABOUT THE AUTHOR

Dear Readers, What you hold in your hands is a message. Some will receive it as poetic, others as revelation, still others as a balm, an ointment of healing for their soul. At the core, the very heart of the message, there is an invitation from God our Father into intimacy with Him, His Son Jesus and His Holy Spirit. In Psalm 42, Vs. 7(NIV), it says "DEEP CALLS TO DEEP", the deep things of God call out the deep things in each of our lives. It is not a shallow, superficial relationship but one that is life changing and eternal. Betty and I first met at our prayer group fellowship several years ago, drawn there by God's grace searching for answers healing and God's love. Since that time we have experienced God's deep love for us and He has grown the seed of who we truly are and who He created us to be.

From that seed grown in Betty the message was born. Psalm 45 Vs. 1 says, "MY MOUTH IS THE PEN OF A READY WRITER" (KJV)

This message was born out of her obedience to God's divine timing, not her own. Her willingness to be patient, to wait for God; to be that ready writer came at the end of the day when she was extremely tired, in the middle of the night or in the wee hours of the morning, during illness, depression, loneliness and in her deliverance of all these things by God.

What you have in your hand is intimacy. Enter in! It is still being birthed. Through the Spirit of Jesus, Brother Jack

Contents

BE STILL AND LISTEN

MY BROTHERS AND SISTERS IN CHRIST
YOU ARE SO SPECIAL TO ME; YOU ARE MY FAMILY
WE ALL COME HERE TO PRAISE OUR GOD
WE ALL COME HERE TO BE SET FREE
THIS IS THE WAY OUR GOD WANTS HIS CHILDREN
TO GATHER TOGETHER TO PRAISE HIS NAME
TO RAISE OUR VOICES IN SONG TO HIM
TO WORSHIP THE ONE WHO TO US CAME
IN THE FORM OF A HELPLESS LITTLE BABE
WHEN HE HEARD OUR MOURNFUL CALL
HE LEFT HIS HEAVENLY THRONE ABOVE
THAT HE MIGHT SAVE US ALL

LET US BE STILL AND LISTEN
THAT WE MAY HEAR OUR SAVIOR SPEAK
FOR HE HAS DONE MIGHTY WORKS FOR US
HE DEFENDS US, FOR WE ARE WEAK
THE ENEMY ATTACKS US FROM EVERY SIDE
BUT OUR MIGHTY GOD WRECKS HIS PLAN
TO STEAL OUR SOULS, TO TURN US AWAY
FROM OUR LORD JESUS, SON OF GOD AND MAN
LET US BE STILL AND LISTEN
FOR OUR GOD HAS MUCH TO GIVE
WE NEED ONLY ASK WITH FAITH AND TRUST
AND WITH HIM WE SHALL FOREVER LIVE

WHEN YOU ARE IN A PLACE OF SOLACE
BE STILL AND LISTEN FOR HIS VOICE
FOR HE WILL SPEAK SOFTLY TO YOUR SOUL
AND IN HIM YOU SHALL REJOICE
HE IS FOREVER WITH US, ALWAYS BY OUR SIDE
AND IF WE FALL FROM HIS HOLY GRACE
IN HIS WOUNDS, HE LETS US HIDE
WHEN WE SHOW SORROW FOR OUR SINS
BECAUSE, IN HIM ONLY, CAN WE LIVE
HE OPENS WIDE HIS SACRED HEART
ALWAYS READY TO FORGIVE

HOLY GOD OF MIGHT

MY CHILDREN, HEAR ME, I WOULD SPEAK MY WORDS THIS NIGHT
IT IS I, YOUR LORD AND SAVIOR, YOUR HOLY GOD OF MIGHT
MY CHILDREN, BEHOLD I COME IN PEACE
MY PEACE I GIVE TO YOU, AND MY LOVE THAT IS TRUE
HOW GOOD AND PLEASANT IT IS FOR ME
TO HEAR YOUR PRAISES SUNG IN UNITY
IT DELIGHTS MY SACRED HEART
AS YOU SING YOUR LOVE FOR ME

WHERE TWO OR MORE ARE GATHERED TOGETHER
IN MY NAME, I AM SURELY IN THEIR MIDST
AS YOU SING YOUR PRAISES TO ME
BE ASSURED THAT I COME BEARING GIFTS
I SHALL GIVE TO YOU, MY BELOVED CHILDREN
ALL THAT YOU ASK FOR WITH FAITH-FILLED HEARTS
BELIEVE IN ME, MY BELOVED ONES
LET NOT YOUR TRUST IN ME DEPART

REMEMBER, MY BELOVED, THAT I AM THE VINE
AND YOU, THE BRANCHES BE
YOU MUST LOVE YOUR GOD WITH ALL YOUR HEART
AND FROM UNHOLY DARKNESS FLEE
I SHALL ALWAYS BE WITH YOU, MY BELOVED ONES
I TAKE MUCH DELIGHT IN YOUR PRAISE
I WILL NOT FAIL NOR FORSAKE THEE
FEAR NOT, NEITHER BE DISMAYED

FOR NOTHING IS TOO HARD FOR YOUR LORD, GOD
CLEVE ONLY, MY CHILDREN, UNTO ME
BEWARE OF THE WICKED ONE, MY CHILDREN
HEED NOT HIS WICKED LIES, NOR LET YOUR HEARTS BE DECEIVED
FEAR NOT, MY LITTLE ONES, COME TO THE LIVING WATER
REMEMBER; NO ONE SHALL COME TO THE FATHER
EXCEPT THROUGH ME, HIS ONLY BEGOTTEN SON
I AM THE ONE TRUE GOD, ALL HOLY AND IMMORTAL ONE

MY BELOVED, KEEP WATCH

MY BELOVED, KEEP WATCH AND BE DILIGENT
FOR I, THE LORD, TELL YOU THAT THE TIME IS NEAR
WHEN YOUR GOD WILL NO LONGER WAIT FOR
HIS UNREPENTANT CHILDREN TO HEAR
THE VOICE OF THEIR GOD WHO OFFERS SALVATION
SO THERE SHALL BE DESTRUCTION OF MANY A NATION
MANY FALSE PROPHETS, TO MY CHILDREN SHALL SPEAK
AND MISLEAD THEM, FOR THEY KNOW THAT THE FLESH IS WEAK
THEY FORGET THAT THEY HAVE THEIR PART TO DO
TO DWELL IN MY KINGDOM, TO HAVE LIFE ANEW

THERE ARE THOSE WHO THINK WITHIN THEIR HEARTS
"JESUS HAS DIED FOR ME AND I AM SAVED, I AM FREE
I AM ALREADY FORGIVEN, I AM ONE SET APART"
TRULY, I SAY, THAT THESE CHILDREN WILL NOT SEE
THE LORD THAT SUFFERED FOR ALL SINNERS' SAKE
FOR THEY HAVE NOT LISTENED, HAVE NOT STAYED AWAKE
MY CHILDREN, TO GAIN PARADISE, TURN AWAY FROM SIN
FOR YOU MUST REPENT IN ORDER TO ENTER IN

YOU KNOW THAT I, YOUR GOD, DID SUFFER ALL
TO RANSOM YOUR SOULS FROM THE EVIL ONE'S CALL
TO MAKE CLEAR THE PATH TO ETERNAL REST
WHERE YOU SHALL GAIN ETERNAL HAPPINESS
MY BELOVED, WHO HEAR ME AND OBEY MY WORD;
WHO HAVE SORROW FOR SIN; YOUR GOD, YOU HAVE HEARD
MY WORD SHALL BE BROUGHT TO ALL THE WORLD'S NATIONS
THAT WITHOUT SINCERE REPENTANCE, THERE IS NO SALVATION

TRULY, I WEEP FOR MY CHILDREN WHO LIVE
BY THE LAW OF THE FLESH, NOT THE LAW OF THEIR GOD
FOR THOSE CHILDREN MAY THINK THAT THEY ARE REDEEMED
BY THE DEATH OF THEIR SAVIOR, THOUGH THEY ARE UNCLEAN
THEY GO OUT INTO THE WORLD, AND LIVE IMPURE LIVES
AND SAY, "I AM SAVED', FOR THEY DON'T REALIZE
THAT FIRST YOU MUST WALK IN THE WAY OF THE LORD
WALK OUT OF THE DARKNESS OR SUFFER THE SWORD
OF DAMNATION, FOR THEY THINK THEY CAN HAVE IT BOTH WAYS
MY BELOVED, KEEP WATCH, BECAUSE I SAVE THOSE WHO PRAY

DO NOT WORRY MY CHILDREN

DO NOT WORRY MY CHILDREN, ABOUT YOUR OWN APPEARANCE
LET THESE FOOLISH THINGS FROM YOUR MIND DEPART
FOR MAN MAY ONLY REGARD OTHERS FROM THE OUTSIDE
WHILE YOUR LORD AND GOD LOOKS UPON YOUR HEART
WHEN MAN LOOKS AT OTHERS; RIGHTEOUSNESS HE MAY SEE,
THOUGH, WITHIN, THEY MAY BE FULL OF HYPOCRISY AND INIQUITY
THE RIGHTEOUS ONES KNOW THAT I AM THE LORD THEIR GOD
AND THE DAY THEY BEHOLD ME, THEY SHALL BE FILLED WITH AWE
FOR I AM YOUR LORD, WHO SEES THE HEARTS OF ALL MEN
I, YOUR GOD, HAVE NO BEGINNING, TO MY EXISTANCE, NO END

I AM IMMORTAL, ALL LOVING, ALMIGHTY, FOR ALL ETERNITY I LIVE
I REMAIN SLOW TO ANGER AND QUICK TO FORGIVE
FOR MY CHILDREN, HATRED STIRRETH UP STRIFES,
BUT LOVE COVERETH ALL SINS, BY MY LOVE DO YOU LIVE
LET NOT ARROGANCY COME OUT OF THY MOUTH,
FOR I AM A GOD OF KNOWLEDGE, AND BY ME, ACTIONS ARE WEIGHED
LOOK NOT UPON THE HAUGHTY, SO THAT YOU MAY BRING HIM DOWN
RATHER LOOK FOR ME IN OTHERS, AND IN MY GRACE, YOU SHALL STAY

THE FOOL HAS SAID IN HIS HEART, 'THERE IS NO GOD'
HE WHO DENIES HIS GOD, IS CONDEMNED BY MY LAW
BUT IF THAT SAME MAN, HAS SORROW AND DECLARES HIS BELIEF
IN HIS GOD WHO MADE HIM, HE SHALL HAVE RELIEF
FOR MY LOVE IS GREATER THAN ALL ETERNITY
MY SHEEP HAS RETURNED, BY MY FORGIVENESS, SET FREE
FOR THOU KNOWEST THY LORD IS FULL OF HOLY GRACE
BY HIS ABUNDANT LOVE, THE LOST HAVE FOUND THEIR PLACE
MY CHILDREN, THOU KNOWEST NOT THE END OF TIME
BE DILIGENT MY CHILDREN, I LOVE YOU, YOU ARE MINE

MY DEARLY BELOVED CHILDREN

MY DEARLY BELOVED, I SHALL NOW SPEAK TO YOU
FROM MY WRITTEN WORDS, WHICH YOU KNOW TO BE TRUE
WHOEVER BELIEVES IN ME, THE ONLY SON OF THE FATHER
BELIEVES IN HIM WHO SENT ME; THEY SHALL COME TO THE WATER
OF LIFE, THEIR SAVIOR, WHO SHOWS THEM THEIR WORTH
BY COMING INTO THE WORLD, BY A VIRGIN BIRTH
FOR WHOEVER SEES ME, SEES ALSO THE ONE WHO SENT ME
FOR I CAME INTO THE WORLD, AS A MOST HOLY LIGHT
AND ALL WHO BELIEVE IN ME AND WHO LOVE ME
SHALL SEE THEIR SAVIOR, WHOSE LOVE IS BURNING BRIGHT
FOR THEN THEY SHALL KNOW THAT THEY HAVE COME
FROM THE DARKNESS OF THE WORLD, TO THE HOLY ONE

ALSO, MY CHILDREN, I, THE SON OF GOD AND MAN
HAVE STRIVED TO MAKE MY LOVED ONES UNDERSTAND
THAT UNLESS YOU BECOME LIKE LITTLE CHILDREN UNTO ME
TO HEAVEN'S DOOR, YOU SHALL NOT FIND THE KEY
DID NOT THE LORD YOUR GOD, GIVE TO YOU THE COMMAND
DO MY CHILDREN, WHOM I LOVE, STILL NOT UNDERSTAND
LOVE THE LORD, YOUR GOD WITH ALL YOUR HEART AND SOUL
THEN YOU SHALL BE BLESSED, YOU SHALL BE WHOLE
LOVE ALSO YOUR NEIGHBOR, AS YOU LOVE YOURSELF
GIVE UNTO THE NEEDY, YES, THE POOR YOU MUST HELP
GIVE UNTO OTHERS, AS MUCH AS YOU ARE ABLE
THEN I SHALL WELCOME YOU TO MY PLENTIFUL TABLE

I, THE LORD, YOUR GOD, SHALL WELCOME THEE
TEARS OF SORROW FOR SIN, SHALL SET YOUR SOULS FREE
FOR ALL THE SINS OF THE WORLD, I CAME AND DIED FOR YOU
ON THE THIRD DAY I ROSE, FOR TO YOU I AM TRUE
IN GLORY, I ROSE FROM THE DEAD; I AM WITH YOU NOW
AT THE SOUND OF MY NAME, HEADS MUST BOW
YOU WHO SUFFER IN TEARS AND SUFFER IN PAIN
TURN TO YOUR SAVIOR WHO BORE THE BLAME
COME UNTO ME, MY BELOVED, I SHALL DRY YOUR TEARS
I SHALL HEAL YOU, BODY AND SOUL, MY CHILDREN, HAVE NO FEAR
LET NO ONE SHAME YOU FOR CALLING ON ME IN YOUR TEARS
YOU ARE MY CHILDREN, MY BELOVED, WHOM I LOVE SO DEAR

THE TEARS I CRIED

MY BELOVED CHILDREN, I MUST LET YOU KNOW THIS
BEFORE I LEFT MY GLORY, MY CROWN, AND MY HEAVENLY BLISS
I, YOUR LORD AND SAVIOR, HAVE COME TO TELL YOU NOW
FROM MY EYES, TEARS I CRIED, MY HOLY HEAD DID BOW
FOR AS IT WAS ORDAINED AND FORETOLD FROM ALL ETERNITY
I MUST SAVE MY PEOPLE; I MUST SET MY CHILDREN FREE
FOR THIS TO BE ACCOMPLISHED, I WOULD TAKE THE FLESH OF MAN
AND SUFFER FOR HIS SINS, ACCORDING TO THE DIVINE PLAN
THE WILL OF THE FATHER WOULD NOW BECOME REALITY
YOUR GOD WOULD COME INTO THE WORLD TO SET THE CAPTIVES FREE

AS FORETOLD IN MY HOLY WORD, A VIRGIN WOULD BEAR A SON
SHE CONCENTED TO BE THE MOTHER OF GOD, THE ONLY BEGOTTEN ONE
AND WHEN THE TIME WAS FULFILLED, IN A STABLE I WAS BORN
TEARS I CRIED AS A LITTLE BABE, FOR MY MOTHER WHO WOULD MOURN
HOW A VIRGIN COULD BEAR A CHILD, ONLY GOD CAN UNDERSTAND
FAITHFUL SERVANT, NOW QUEEN OF HEAVEN, OF ANGELS, AND OF MAN
FOR DIVINITY AND MAN WAS MIXED BY THE HOLY SPIRIT'S POWER
THE WORD MADE FLESH WAS BORN TO A HUMBLE VIRGIN FLOWER
YOUR LORD GREW INTO MANHOOD TO PAY THE WAGES OF SIN
YES I WOULD DIE UPON THE CROSS TO USHER REDEMPTION IN

THINK NOT, MY BELOVED CHILDREN, THOSE TEARS WERE CRIED FOR ME
BUT FOR UNREPENTANT SINNERS, YOUR LORD WEPT BITTERLY
FOR I KNEW FROM THE BEGINNING, NOT ALL WOULD, TO ME, TURN
IT WAS FOR WORDLY TREASURES, AND NOT FOR GOD THEY YEARNED
TO SAVE MY CHILDREN FROM ETERNAL DEATH, I DIED ON CALVARY
BUT MAN MUST ACCEPT MY HOLY GIFT OF DEATH UPON A TREE
REPENT OF SIN, WORSHIP YOUR GOD, COME AND FOLLOW THE HOLY ONE
FOR NO ONE SEES THE FATHER, EXCEPT THROUGH HIS BLESSED SON
TEARS I CRIED, NOT FROM FEAR OF DEATH,, BUT FOR UNREPENTANT SOULS
WHO FAIL TO ACCEPT THEIR SAVIOR, FROM WHOM LIVING WATER FLOWS

MY DELIGHT IS IN MY CHILDREN

OH MY BELOVED CHILDREN, MY VERY OWN
I TAKE SUCH DELIGHT IN YOUR SONGS OF PRAISE
THEY RISE UP TO THE HEAVEN'S DOME
MY HEART FILLS WITH JOY, AS YOUR HANDS YOU RAISE
KNOW THAT MY LOVE IS EVERLASTING
A DEEP, ABIDING LOVE, FAR SURPASSING
ANY LOVE IN HEAVEN, ANY LOVE ON EARTH
YOU ARE MY TREASURE, YOU HAVE ENDLESS WORTH
RIGHTLY YOU GIVE YOUR PRAISES TO ME
FOR I AM THE ONE WHO SETS YOU FREE
PRAISE FOR YOUR SAVIOR IS PRAISE FOR YOUR FATHER
AND PRAISE FOR OUR HOLY SPIRIT, FOR ONE GOD ARE WE

JUST AS MY LOVE IS EVERLASTING, MY CHILDREN
SO IS THE COVENANT I MADE WITH THEE
FOR I AM THE WAY, THE TRUTH AND THE LIFE
NO ONE COMES TO THE FATHER EXCEPT THROUGH ME
SO RAISE YOUR VOICES, LIFT YOUR HEARTS
I TAKE DELIGHT IN YOUR SONGS OF PRAISE
KNOW THAT I AM WITH YOU FOR ALL DAYS
BRINGING SHOWERS OF MY BLESSINGS AND GRACE
ANGELS JOIN IN YOUR PRAISES ON HIGH
AS YOUR VOICES FILL THE SKIES
WHEN YOU SHOW YOUR FAITH IN ONLY ME
FROM AFFLICTIONS, I SHALL SURELY SET YOU FREE

I COME TO YOU WITH A LOVING HEART
YES, MY SACRED HEART BURNS WITH JOY
FOR I KNOW MY CHILDREN, AND THEY KNOW ME
I WANT TO GIVE TO THEM ABUNDANTLY
FREELY I GIVE AND FREELY I LOVE
MY HEALING POWERS ARE WITHOUT END
JUST ASK ME WITH EXPECTANT FAITH
TURN TO YOUR SAVIOR, FOR I AM YOUR FRIEND
AND IF YOU SHOULD SOMETIMES OFFEND YOUR GOD
HAVE SORROW, AND FORGIVENESS, YOU SHALL RECEIVE
FOR MY LOVE AND MY MERCY HAVE NO END
DO THE SAME FOR THOSE WHO HAVE OFFENDED THEE

COME BACK TO ME

THIS IS WHAT I WANT OF YOU, MY PEOPLE
THIS IS WHAT YOU MUST DO, MY PEOPLE
SPEAK THESE WORDS TO ALL MY LITTLE ONES
'REPENT AND BE SAVED, MY WILL BE DONE'
DO NOT BE AFRAID MY CHILDREN, COME KNOCK ON MY DOOR
YOU WILL BE BID TO ENTER TO LOVE FOREVERMORE

BE STILL AND LISTEN TO MY HOLY TRUTH
YOUR SAVING LORD HAS NOT FORSAKEN YOU
I HAVE COME TO RECLAIM THE LOST
WHO HAVE BEEN REDEEMED BY MY HOLY CROSS
COME BACK TO ME, TURN AWAY FROM SIN
I AM THE GATE WHERE YOU MAY ENTER IN

I KNOW ALL YOUR FAULTS AND FAILINGS
I KNOW THE ENEMY IS CALLING TO YOU
YOU MUST REBUKE HIM IN MY NAME
FOR I WILL SEND HIM FROM WHENCE HE CAME
ALL YOU NEED TO DO, MY CHILDREN,
IS TO CALL ON MY HOLY NAME

BE NOT AFRAID MY LITTLE ONES, I WANT TO SET YOU FREE
TO WELCOME YOU INTO MY KINGDOM
MY BELOVED, COME UNTO ME
YOU NEED, BUT PUT YOUR TRUST AND FAITH
IN THE WAY THE TRUTH AND THE LIFE
I SHALL WIPE AWAY YOUR TEARS, FREE YOU FROM ALL STRIFE

TURN AWAY FROM THE DREADFUL DARKNESS
FOR ONLY, I, AM LOVE AND LIGHT
I AM YOUR GOD, COME WALK WITH ME
FOR WITH ME THERE IS NO NIGHT
THERE IS NOTHING YOUR LORD CAN'T FORGIVE OF YOU
FOR MY LOVE IS ETERNAL AND IS TRUE

I, YOUR GOD, HAVE PAID THE PRICE TO SET MY CHILDREN FREE
I ALONE, AM YOUR SAVIOR, TAKE UP YOUR CROSS AND FOLLOW ME
LISTEN TO MY WORDS, MY BELOVED, FOR ONLY I, AND I ALONE
CAN BRING YOU OUT OF THE DARKNESS TO WORSHIP AT MY THRONE
OH MY LITTLE CHILDREN, HARKEN UNTO ME
THEN YOU WILL COME TO MY KINGDOM FOR ALL ETERNITY

MY BELOVED CHILDREN

MY BELOVED CHILDREN, PAY HEED TO WHAT YOUR GOD HAS TO SAY
KNOW THAT THE WAYS OF THE LORD, CAN NOT BE AS YOUR WAYS
THINK NOT, THAT I DO NOT HEAR YOUR MOURNFUL CRIES
MY BELOVED, OPEN YOUR HEART TO ME AND OPEN YOUR EYES
KNOW THAT MY KNOWLEDGE AND WISDOM IS BEYOND INFINITY
KNOW ALSO YOUR GOD, MY CHILDREN, AS THE BLESSED TRINITY
I, YOUR HEAVENLY FATHER, WILL BLESS YOU BEYOND MEASURE
IF ONLY IN YOUR HEART, MY LIVING WORD YOU TREASURE

I, THE SON, HAVE PROVEN MY ENDLESS LOVE FOR YOU
THEREFORE, YOU MUST FOLLOW ME, IN WHATEVER YOU MAY DO
I AM THE LIVING WORD, YOU MUST TREASURE IN YOUR HEART
MY HOLY SPIRIT I HAVE SENT; FROM YOU HE'LL NOT DEPART
FOR THE SPIRIT DOTH PROCEED FROM THE FATHER AND THE SON
MY CHILDREN, WE THREE DIVINE, ARE YOUR GOD, THE ONLY ONE
LET YOUR EYES, LIGHT OF YOUR BODY, PERCEIVE FIRST, ONLY ME
AND I, YOUR ONE AND ONLY GOD, WILL SET YOUR SPIRIT FREE

TRUST THE LORD WITH ALL YOUR HEART IN ALL THAT YOU MAY DO
REMEMBER GOD, THROUGH HIS BELOVED SON, HAS FORGIVEN YOU
BE KIND TO ONE ANOTHER AND REMEMBER TO FORGIVE
A FAITHFUL FRIEND, AND LOVING HEART, ETERNALLY SHALL LIVE
GIVE TO THE LESS FORTUNATE, GIVE WITH A CHEERFUL HEART
FOR HE THAT GIVETH, RECEIVETH, FOR HE HAS DONE HIS PART
TO SPREAD THE LOVE OF GOD, BY HIS ACTIONS AND GOOD DEEDS
HE SHARES GOD'S HOLY LIGHT, THE HUNGRY HE DOTH FEED

I AM LOVE ETERNAL, FOR YOU, MY CHILDREN, MY LOVE IS DEEP
I LOVE YOU WHEN YOU ARE AWAKE, I LOVE YOU AS YOU SLEEP
MY GOODNESS AND MY MERCY, FOREVER I SHALL YIELD
I SHALL BE YOUR FORTRESS, AND I SHALL BE YOUR SHIELD
FEAR NOT THE DECEIVER, WHEN YOU ARE WALKING IN MY GRACE
FOR I, YOUR LORD, SHALL BANISH THE SERPANT TO HIS PLACE
AND I, THE LAMB, WHICH IS IN THE MIDST OF THE GREAT THRONE
SHALL ALWAYS AND EVER STRIVE TO BRING MY CHILDREN HOME.

HOLY FIRE

HOLY FIRE, COME TO ME
CLEANSE MY SOUL AND SET ME FREE
HOLY SPIRIT, ENTER IN
LET ME NEVER FALL IN SIN
STAY MY JESUS, BY MY SIDE
IN THY HOLY WOUNDS, LET ME HIDE
GOD, MY FATHER, I THANK THEE
YOU SENT YOUR SON TO RESCUE ME
JESUS, FROM YOUR SACRED HEART
LET ME NEVER BE APART

JESUS, WHO IS LOVE AND LIGHT
SHELTER ME FROM THE DARK NIGHT
SONG OF JUSTICE, FOREVER REIGN
LOVE BURN IN MY HEART AGAIN
EASE MY BURDENS, DRY MY TEARS
FILL ME WITH YOUR HOLY FEAR
KEEP ME ALWAYS CLOSE TO THEE
MY SALVATION, HEAVEN'S KEY

JESUS, SAVIOR, BURNING BRIGHT
IN YOUR WORD, MY SOUL DELIGHTS
MAY I ALWAYS TURN TO THEE
FROM MY PAIN, LORD, SET ME FREE
WHEN MY DAYS ON EARTH ARE THROUGH
MAY MY SPIRIT FLEE TO YOU
TO SERVE MY GOD, MY ONE DESIRE
FILL ME WITH YOUR HOLY FIRE

I SAW JESUS

I SAW JESUS TODAY, HE WAS COLD, FOR HE HAD NO COAT
I GAVE HIM A BLANKET TO WEAR
HE SMILED AT ME AND SAID 'THANK YOU'
THEN I SAW THAT HIS FEET WERE BARE
SO I LOOKED TO TRY TO FIND
WARM STOCKINGS AND SHOES; HIS FACE DID SHINE
THEN I SAW THAT HE MUST BE HUNGRY
FOR HE WAS THIN AND HE LOOKED WEAK
I GAVE HIM FOOD, THEN HE TOUCHED MY CHEEK

I KNEW THAT I HAD SEEN HIM BEFORE
A SICK LITTLE CHILD WHO WAS IN NEED
WITH LOVING CARE, I GAVE HIM ALL I HAD
TILL FROM THE SICKNESS HE WAS FREED
WHEN HE AWAKENED, HE WAS THIRSTY
SO I GAVE HIM WATER TO DRINK
THEN THE SMILE ON HIS FACE WAS, OH, SO BRIGHT
IT BANISHED THE DARKNESS AND BANISHED THE NIGHT

I WILL VISIT JESUS IN PRISON TODAY
A TROUBLED TEEN, WHO HAS LOST HIS WAY
HE NEEDS TO BE SHOWN HOW TO DEAL WITH STRIFE
SO THAT WITH THE LORD, HE WILL HAVE LIFE
MY BROTHERS AND SISTERS WHEN YOU GO ABOUT
IF YOU SEE ONE IN NEED, TRY TO HELP HIM OUT
FOR OUR JESUS SAID IN HIS HOLY WORD
LOVE THY NEIGHBOR AND THY PRAYERS SHALL SURELY BE HEARD
FOR WHATSOEVER THOU SHALT DO UNTO THE LEAST OF THESE
MY BELOVED CHILDREN, YOU DO UNTO ME

COME MY CHILDREN, COME

COME MY CHILDREN, COME TO THE LIVING WATERS
THAT FLOW ENDLESSLY, ETERNALLY
MY BELOVED CHILDREN, COME
COME MY CHILDREN, COME TO THE FEAST,
THE FEAST THAT CELEBRATES MY LOVE FOR YOU
MY BELOVED CHILDREN, COME
COME MY CHILDREN, COME TO THE FATHER
ONLY THROUGH YOUR SAVIOR, CAN YOU BEHOLD HIM
MY BELOVED CHILDREN, COME
COME MY CHILDREN, COME TO THE LIVING WORD
WHO CONQUERED DEATH AND SIN
MY BELOVED CHILDREN, COME

COME MY CHILDREN, COME TO THE PLENTIFUL TABLE
WHERE YOU WILL FIND FOOD FOR LIFE
MY BELOVED CHILDREN, COME
COME MY CHILDREN, COME TO LOVE ETERNAL
ONLY IN YOUR LORD SHALL YOU FIND IT
MY BELOVED CHILDREN, COME
COME MY CHILDREN, COME TO EVERLASTING JOY
MY HOLY SPIRIT SHALL LEAD YOU
MY BELOVED CHILDREN, COME
COME MY CHILDREN, COME TO THE FOOT OF MY CROSS
WHERE YOU MAY LAY YOUR BURDENS DOWN
MY BELOVED CHILDREN, COME

COME MY CHILDREN, BE WASHED BY MY SACRED BLOOD
WHICH I FREELY SHED FOR YOU, MY LITTLE ONES
MY BELOVED CHILDREN, COME
COME MY CHILDREN, COME PARTAKE OF MY SACRED BODY
WHICH I FREELY GAVE UNTO DEATH FOR YOU
MY BELOVED CHILDREN, COME
COME MY CHILDREN, COME WALK IN THE LIGHT OF YOUR SAVIOR
WHO BANISHES ALL DARKNESS AND FEAR
MY BELOVED CHILDREN, COME
COME MY CHILDREN, ALL YE WHO SEEK THE WAY
THE TRUTH AND THE LIFE
COME TO ME, MY BELOVED CHILDREN, COME

AS IT IS WRITTEN

AS IT IS WRITTEN, LET IT BE TOLD, ISAIAH SPOKETH TRUE
IN PROPHECY IT WAS FORETOLD OF A COVENANT NEW
GOD SPOKE THROUGH HIS PROPHETS OF HIS DIVINE PLAN
HIS ONLY BEGOTTEN SON WOULD TAKE THE FLESH OF MAN

AS T'WAS FORETOLD; IN GOD'S OWN TIME, A HUMBLE VIRGIN PURE
OBEYED HER GOD ALMIGHTY, HIS WILL SHE DID SECURE
ANGEL GABRIEL TOLD HER HOW GOD WOULD BECOME MAN
SHE SAID "LET IT BE DONE UNTO ME, ACCORDING TO THY PLAN."

THEN BY THE POWER OF THE HOLY SPIRIT, OF OUR ALMIGHTY LORD
THE LIVING WORD WOULD COME TO EARTH, A KING TO BE ADORED
A VIRGIN BIRTH, AS T'WAS FORETOLD, SHE WAS TO BRING FORTH A SON
HE WOULD BE THE SON OF GOD AND MAN, GOD'S ONLY BEGOTTEN ONE

NOT IN A STATELY PALACE, BUT IN A STABLE BARE AND COLD
MARY'S LITTLE BABY BOY WAS BORN, AS IT WAS FORETOLD
JOSEPH, MARY'S SPOUSE, WAS TOLD, THAT WHEN THE BABY CAME
THE ONLY BEGOTTEN SON OF GOD, "JESUS" WOULD BE HIS NAME

THE ANGELS SANG, THE SHEPHERDS CAME AND FOLLOWING A STAR,
CAME THE WISEMEN, THREE GREAT KINGS, WHO HAD TRAVELLED FAR
THEY SET BEFORE THE HOLY CHILD, GOLD, FRANKENCENSE AND MIRRH
THEY GAZED UPON THE LITTLE BABE, THEIR MIGHTY HEARTS ASTIR

BROTHERS AND SISTERS REJOICE, BE GLAD, ON THIS DECEMBER DAY
FOR WAS BORN THE LORD OUR SAVIOR, WHO IN A MANGER LAY
AS IT WAS IN THE BEGINNING, IS NOW AND SHALL EVER BE
THE LIVING WORD HATH COME TO EARTH, TO SET THE CAPTIVES FREE

THUS SAYS THE LORD; I AM

*I AM GOD OF THE UNIVERSE, THE SUPREME
CREATOR OF THINGS SEEN AND UNSEEN
THE HEAVENS, THE EARTH AND ALL ON IT AND IN IT
OCEANS, MOUNTAINS AND SKY WITHOUT LIMIT
IN MY OWN IMAGE DID I CREATE MAN
I REIGN OVER ALL BECAUSE I CAN
I AM YOUR GOD, THE LORD OF ALL
THE GREAT 'I AM', ON WHOM YOU CALL*

*THE SON OF MAN, I AM HE
AT THE SOUND OF MY NAME, ALL BEND THEIR KNEE
FOR ALL CREATION, I DESCENDED FROM ABOVE
TO SHOW THE WORLD THAT GOD IS LOVE
I CAME, NOT TO CONDEMN, BUT TO SAVE
I AM YOUR KING WHO BECAME A SLAVE
IT WAS I WHO CAME AS A SACRIFICIAL LAMB
I DID THESE THINGS BECAUSE 'I AM'*

*I AM THE HOLY SPIRIT, SENT BY THE TWO
I AM SENT HERE TO SANCTIFY YOU
I AM HERE AS YOUR COMFORT, AND HERE AS YOUR GUIDE
WITH THE FATHER AND THE SON, I ABIDE
I AM IN THEM, AS THEY ARE IN ME
ONE GOD ONLY, WITH DIVINE PERSONS, THREE
IF YOU ARE SEARCHING FOR THE SAVIOR OF MAN
LOOK TO ME, YOUR GOD, BECAUSE 'I AM'*

FEAR NOT, MY CHILDREN

MY BELOVED CHILDREN, I WILL SPEAK TO YOU
TO LET YOU KNOW THAT MY LOVE IS TRUE
I AM WITH YOU FOREVER, YES, TILL THE END OF TIME
IT IS FOR YOU I YEARN, FOR YOU ARE MINE
MY HEAVENLY FATHER GAVE YOU UNTO ME
SO THAT YOU MAY LIVE ETERNALLY
FOR I HAVE OBEYED HIS LOVING COMMAND
TOOK ON YOUR FLESH AND BECAME MAN

I DWELT WITH YOU, THOUGH I AM YOUR LORD
THE KING OF KINGS, TO BE ADORED
YET; I FORSOOK MY HEAVENLY THRONE
I LIVED FOR YOU, AND YOU ALONE
MY WOUNDS WERE MANY, AND GREAT WAS MY PAIN
FOR YOUR SALVATION, I TOOK THE BLAME
I WAS CRUSHED AND TORN, AND GLADLY, I DIED
TO SAVE MY CHILDREN, MYSELF, I DENIED

MY CHILDREN, FEAR NOT, FOR THOUGH I DIED
I CONQUERED SIN AND DEATH AND I AM ALIVE
I DWELL IN YOU AND YOU DWELL IN ME
BECAUSE YOU ARE MINE, I SET YOU FREE
FREE FROM SIN, FREE FROM DEATH
FOLLOW ME, MY CHILDREN; THEN YOU SHALL HAVE REST
CLAIM YOUR LORD, AS YOUR SAVIOR, BE SORRY FOR SIN
THEN, TO HEAVEN'S GLORY, YOU SHALL ENTER IN

SO LIFT UP YOUR VOICES, PRAISE MY HOLY NAME
BECAUSE, FOR YOU, I BORE THE SHAME
LIFT UP YOUR HANDS TOWARD MY THRONE
FOR YOU KNOW NOT WHEN I SHALL CALL YOU HOME,
AND KNOW THAT IF YOU CALL ON MY HOLY NAME
I SHALL EASE YOUR BURDENS, AND EASE YOUR PAIN
KEEP WATCH, MY CHILDREN, GIVE YOUR HEART TO ME
FOR I AM EVER READY, TO SET YOU FREE

Elizabeth Ann Marks

JESUS, LIVING WATER

OH GOOD JESUS, LIVING WATER EVER FLOWING
WASHING AWAY THE SINS OF YOUR CHILDREN
LET OUR FAITH BE EVER GROWING
PRECIOUS SAVIOR, LAMB OF GOD
WONDERFUL COUNCELOR, EVER TEACHING
TO YOUR WAYWARD CHILDREN, EVER REACHING
YOUR CEASELESS, ENDLESS LOVE, YOU POUR
BOUNDLESS MERCY, MORE AND MORE

YOU ARE GOD, THE MIGHTY KING ON HIGH
YET, FOR OUR SAKES, YOU CHOSE TO DIE
YOU LOVED US, YOUR CHILDREN, THE LOST
CONCENTED TO SUFFER UPON THE CROSS
THOUGH UNJUSTLY JUDGED, YOU BORE THE SHAME
FOR YOUR SINFUL CHILDREN, YOU TOOK THE BLAME
OH MY SAVIOR, WHATEVER CAN IT BE
THAT YOU, WILLINGLY, HAVE NOT DONE FOR ME

WITHOUT YOUR EVER FLOWING WATER, MY LORD
LIVING WATER, SO GENEROUSLY POURED
OVER OUR SOULS, TO WASH AWAY
OUR GREVIOUS SINS, DAY BY DAY
WHERE WOULD YOUR WAYWARD CHILDREN BE
WITHOUT YOUR MERCY, TO SET US FREE
YOUR WORD; IT IS OUR FOOD FOR LIFE
YOUR GLORIOUS PRESENCE AND HOLY LIGHT

OH LIVING WATER, HOLY LIVING BREAD
GLORIOUS SAVIOR, BY WHOM WE ARE FED
WE TURN TO YOU, LORD, FOR YOU ARE OUR GOD
YOU SHED YOUR BLOOD, WITHSTOOD THE ROD
YOU CONCENTED TO DIE, BUT GLORIOUSLY ROSE
THE WILL OF YOUR HEAVENLY FATHER, YOU CHOSE
YOU ARE LIVING WATER, FLOWING EVER FREE
TO QUENCH OUR THIRST AND BRING US TO THEE

ALL IS RIGHT WITH YOUR SOUL

MY CHILDREN, I, YOUR LORD, AM HERE TO TELL YOU
THAT I LOVE YOU SO VERY DEEPLY, I AM GLAD YOU ARE MINE
MY CHILDREN, THERE IS STILL MUCH WORK WE MUST DO
AND I SHALL CONTINUE TO ACCOMPLISH MUCH, THROUGH YOU
FOR I SEEK THE CHILDREN WHO HAVE STRAYED FROM ME
SO THAT WHEN THEIR DAYS ON EARTH HAVE ENDED
TOGETHER, WE SHALL SET THEM FREE
MY CHILDREN, FAITHFUL SERVANTS, YOU ARE BLESSED BY ME

YOU MUST KEEP DOING THE WORK I HAVE GIVEN YOU
AND TO YOUR LORD, YOU MUST CONTINUE TO BE TRUE
MANY ARE THE BLESSINGS, I HOLD FOR EACH ONE
OF MY CHILDREN WHO SEE THAT MY WILL BE DONE
YOU DO AS ALL MY SERVANTS STRIVE TO DO
WHICH IS PUTTING OTHER'S NEEDS BEFORE YOUR OWN
YOU ARE ON THE STRAIGHT PATH, TO YOUR HEAVENLY HOME
WHERE YOU SHALL REJOICE AROUND MY GREAT THRONE

YOU HAVE SET OTHERS FREE FROM PAIN AND DOUBT
YOU HAVE CALLED ON ME TO FULFILL THEIR NEEDS
FOR YOU KNOW WHAT DOING THE WILL OF GOD IS ABOUT
THOSE FREED BY YOUR SAVING LORD, ARE FREE INDEED
KNOW, ALSO, THAT TO SEE THE FATHER, YOU MUST GO TO THE SON
FOR YOU ARE HEIRS WITH THE MOST HOLY ONE
YOU WHO WORK THROUGH THE SPIRIT, HEAVEN IS YOUR GOAL
I AM PLEASED TO TELL YOU, ALL IS RIGHT WITH YOUR SOUL

YOU, MY CHILDREN, ARE SO VERY SPECIAL TO ME
YOU HAVE SET MANY OF YOUR BROTHERS AND SISTERS FREE
YOU HAVE CAST OUT THEIR PAIN IN MY NAME; 'JESUS CHRIST'
YOU ARDENTLY WORK TO SHOW THEM MY HOLY LIGHT
THE COMFORTER, MY SPIRIT, WHICH LEADS YOU IN THESE TASKS
KNOWS I SHALL GIVE EVERYTHING, THAT, IN MY NAME, YOU ASK
MY CHILDREN, WORK DILIGENTLY, TO ATTAIN THAT GOAL
AND KNOW THAT WITH ME, ALL IS RIGHT WITH YOUR SOUL

Elizabeth Ann Marks

I SHALL PLACE MY TRUST IN THE LORD

AS YOU TELL ME IN PROVERBS THREE, VERSES FIVE AND SIX, MY GOD
I SHALL TRUST IN YOU, THE LORD, WITH ALL MY HEART
I SHALL NOT LEAN ON MY OWN UNDERSTANDING
LEAD ME IN YOUR WAYS, LORD, FROM THEM, MAY I NOT DEPART

AND IN MATTHEW SEVEN YOU TELL ME TO ASK
AND IT SHALL BE GIVEN UNTO ME, SEEK AND I SHALL FIND
KNOCK AND THE DOOR SHALL BE OPENED UNTO ME, OH LORD
BURN YOUR HOLY WORDS ON MY HEART AND ON MY MIND

FOR ALL THAT ASK SHALL RECEIVE, ALL THAT SEEK, SHALL FIND THEE
BEHOLD, I KNOCK, OH PRECIOUS SAVIOR, LET THE DOOR OPEN UNTO ME
YOUR WORD TELLS ME, LORD, TO GIVE; IT'S A LESSON WE MUST ALL LEARN
WHAT MEASURE GIVEN UNTO OTHERS SHALL BE DEALT UNTO US IN RETURN

LET YOUR WORDS BE FOREVER IMPRINTED, IN MY HEART AND SOUL
FOR YOUR HOLY WISDOM, LORD, LET ME FOREVER YEARN
MAY I NOT BE AFRAID, MY GOD, FOR YOU ARE ALWAYS WITH ME
IN YOUR LIGHT MAY I EVER WALK; MAY MY LOVE FOR YOU EVER BURN

DEPART NOT FROM MY SIDE, OH LORD, MY GOD, WHO SETS ME FREE
IN YOUR ENDLESS MERCY, LORD, BEHOLD ME AS YOUR OWN
GRANT UNTO ME PATIENCE, LOVE AND FORGIVENESS, MY SAVIOR,
RECALL YOUR HOLY SACRIFICE TO BRING YOUR SERVANT HOME

KING OF THE WORLD

BEHOLD, MY CHILDREN, MY LITTLE ONES
THE KING OF THE WORLD IS IN YOUR MIDST
THE LORD, YOUR GOD, HAS PROMISED YOU THIS
THAT WHERESOEVER TWO OR MORE
GATHER TOGETHER IN MY HOLY NAME
I SHALL COME TO HEAL YOU, TO TAKE AWAY YOUR PAIN
SO, MY CHILDREN, ASK, FOR I WANT TO GIVE
IT IS I WHO DIED, SO THAT YOU MIGHT LIVE
THERE ARE SO MANY GIFTS THAT I HAVE FOR YOU
PLACE YOUR TRUST IN ME, I SHALL CARRY YOU THROUGH
FOR I, WHO ROSE IN GLORY, WHO DEFEATED DEATH
AND DEFEATED SIN, YES, I SHALL GIVE YOU REST

I HAVE SOLEMNLY SWORN, BY MY MOST HOLY NAME
NEVER TO ABANDON MY CHILDREN, MY LOVE IS A FLAME
BURNING BRIGHTLY TO LIGHT YOUR WAY
SO THAT FROM THE PATH YOU DO NOT STRAY
FOR I AM THE WAY, THE TRUTH AND THE LIFE
COME TO ME, LITTLE ONES, FOR I AM THE LIGHT
I AM YOUR SAVIOR, YOUR BROTHER, YOUR GUIDE
WALK WITH ME, I SHALL EVER BE BY YOUR SIDE
WHATSOEVER YOU MAY ASK OF ME WITH CHILDLIKE TRUST
I, YOUR GOD, SHALL GIVE, FOR NOTHING IS IMPOSSIBLE WITH ME
DID I NOT FASHION YOU FROM THE VERY DUST?
TRULY, I AM YOUR GOD, WHO NOW SETS YOU FREE

FOR I LOVE YOU, MY CHILDREN, WITH A DEEP, DEEP LOVE
I HAVE COME TO YOU WITH ARMS STRETCHED WIDE
TO HOLD MY CHILDREN, FOR WHOM I LONG
TO GUIDE AND PROTECT; IN MY WOUNDS YOU SHALL HIDE
I SHALL CREATE IN YOU, MY CHILDREN, A CLEAN, PURE HEART
SO THAT FROM YOUR LORD, YOU SHALL NOT DEPART
THOUGH KING OF THE WORLD, OF HEAVEN AND EARTH
CREATOR OF ALL THINGS ,HERE AND BEYOND THIS UNIVERSE
MY SPIRIT I HAVE BREATHED INTO YOU, MY LITTLE ONES
I AM KING OF THE WORLD, MY WILL SHALL BE DONE
I SHALL PROTECT MY BELOVED FROM THE ONE WHO DECEIVES
FOR THE EVIL ONE HAS NO POWER OVER ME

JOYFULLY WE SING

OH GOOD AND GENTLE JESUS, PUREST JOY OF MY LIFE
I THANK THEE EXCEEDINGLY FOR BRINGING ME HERE TONIGHT
SO THAT I MAY, WITH MY BROTHERS AND SISTERS,
SING PRAISES TO THEE; BE PRESENT IN THY HOLY LIGHT
IT IS RIGHT TO GIVE THEE THANKS AND PRAISE
TO JOYFULLY EXALT THY MOST HOLY NAME
FOR MANY THE GIFTS YOU BESTOW ON US
MANY THE SINS, FOR WHICH YOU BORE THE BLAME

WE LOVE TO SING YOUR PRAISES, OH LORD, OUR VERY BREATH
WHO TAKES AWAY THE SINS OF THE WHOLE WORLD
AND SAVES HIS CHILDREN FROM ETERNAL DEATH
JOYFULLY WE SING TO YOU WHO CAME WITH ARMS UNFURLED
AND FOR THE SINS OF YOUR CHILDREN, YOU CAME TO PAY THE PRICE
BECAUSE YOU ARE OUR LORD, THE MESSIAH AND THE CHRIST
YOU TRADED YOUR HEAVENLY GLORY AND YOUR PRECIOUS CROWN
FOR ONE MADE OF THORNS, MOST CRUELLY PRESSED DOWN

OH LORD, STILL, YOU GIVE ABUNDANTLY TO YOUR CHILDREN
GIFTS OF MERCY, GIFTS OF FORGIVENESS, HEALING AND LOVE
IN YOUR WOUNDS, YOU GRACIOUSLY HIDE US
JESUS, LIVING WORD SENT FROM HEAVEN ABOVE
YOU MEEKLY BORE THE HEAVY CROSS THAT DAY ON CALVARY
YOU DIED AND GLORIOUSLY ROSE AGAIN, TO SET THE CAPTIVES FREE
PRAISE TO YOU, OH PRECIOUS JESUS, MOST HOLY, GLORIOUS LIGHT
JOYFULLY WE SING TO YOU, THE WAY, THE TRUTH AND THE LIFE

WE HAVE NOTHING WITHOUT OUR LORD

WE MAY HAVE RICHES IN THIS WORLD
WE HAVE NOTHING WITHOUT OUR LORD
WE MAY BE FAMOUS IN THIS WORLD
WE HAVE NOTHING WITHOUT OUR LORD
OUR LIVES MAY BE FILLED WITH EXCITING THINGS
WE HAVE NOTHING WITHOUT OUR LORD
IF WE DO NOT FIRST, HAVE LOVE,
WE HAVE NOTHING WITHOUT OUR LORD

SO BOAST NOT OF YOUR EARTHLY RICHES
BOAST NOT OF THOSE WORLDLY THINGS
YOU MUST BUILD YOUR TREASURES IN HEAVEN
ONLY THEN, WILL YOUR HEART TAKE WINGS
LISTEN TO THE HOLY WORD
GIVEN TO US, FROM THE LORD ON HIGH
WHO SENT HIS ONLY BEGOTTEN SON
WHO DID, FOR LOVE'S SAKE, CHOOSE TO DIE

IF YOU WANT THE TRUEST TREASURES
CLAIM THE SAVIOR FOR YOUR OWN
ONLY IN HIM CAN WE TRULY LIVE
LIFE ETERNAL, AT HIS HEAVENLY THRONE
WE MUST TURN AWAY FROM DARKNESS
AND IN HIS LIGHT WE MUST EVER BE
BY HIS LIFE, DEATH AND RESURRECTION
HE CLEANSED OUR SOULS AND SET US FREE

SO NOW WE MUST PUT OUR GOD FIRST
LOVE NOT THE WORLD, BUT OUR SAVING LORD
FATHER, SON AND HOLY SPIRIT
HOLY OF HOLIES, MUCH ADORED
SHOW YOUR LOVE FOR YOUR NEIGHBOR
HELP THE POOR, THE LONELY, THE STRESSED
FOR WHATSOEVER WE DO FOR THEM
WE DO FOR OUR SAVIOR, AND WE SHALL BE BLESSED

SO WORSHIP NOT FALSE GODS OF RICHES
KEEP JESUS TREASURED IN YOUR HEART
MAY HIS SACRED HEART BE EVER ADORED
FROM HIM, MAY WE NEVER BE APART
LET OUR HEARTS BURN WITH LOVE FOR HIM
NOT EARTHLY TREASURES, WE MAY HAVE STORED
FOR THOUGH WE MAY HAVE EARTHLY RICHES
WE HAVE NOTHING WITHOUT OUR LORD.

OH GLORIOUS LIGHT

OH LORD, YOU ARE ALL GLORIOUS LIGHT
FOR THE WHOLE WORLD TO SEE
YOU GAVE YOUR ALL WITH LOVE AND MIGHT
YOUR TRUTH HAS SET US FREE
OH GLORIOUS FATHER IN HEAVEN
OUR GOD BY NIGHT AND BY DAY
YOU SENT YOUR PRECIOUS SON
TO WASH OUR SINS AWAY

JESUS SUFFERED AND SHED HIS SACRED BLOOD
FOR ALL SINNERS HE BORE THE BLAME
TO GIVE US LIFE ETERNAL
PRAISE, OH PRAISE HIS HOLY NAME
WITH HEAD BOWED LOW, HE MEEKLY BORE
SHAME THAT WAS NOT HIS
WITH A HEAVY CROSS UPON HIS SHOULDER
NO OTHER COULD DO SUCH AS THIS

OH HOLY ONE, REDEEMER LORD;
AN ANCIENT PROMISE TO FULFULL
OH INNOCENT LAMB YOU MEEKLY WALKED
TO DEATH UPON THAT HILL
OH WORTHY ONE, OH GLORUS GOD
WITH MEEKNESS AND WITH MIGHT
TO SAVE THE LOST, YOU BORE THE CROSS
OUT OF DARKNESS, CAME GLORIOUS LIGHT

IN GLORY, LORD, YOU ROSE AGAIN
AGAIN, WE PRAISE YOUR HOLY NAME
YOU WHO ARE OUR ONE TRUE GOD
STEPPED UP, AND BORE THE BLAME
YOU CONQUERED DEATH, YOU CONQUERED SIN
SAVED US FROM THE DARKEST NIGHT
YOU BOUGHT US LIFE, YOU SET US FREE
TO SHARE IN YOUR GLORIOUS LIGHT

LORD, WE, YOUR CHILDREN

LORD, WE YOUR CHILDREN, DESIRE MUCH MORE
AS BLESSINGS FROM YOUR THRONE YOU POUR
GIVE TO US YOUR SAVING GRACE
WE LONG TO SEE YOUR HOLY FACE
COVER US WITH YOUR PRECIOUS BLOOD
THAT WE MAY NOT PERISH IN THE FLOOD
OF GRIEF AND SORROW, PAIN AND SIN
LET NOT THE ENEMY ENTER IN

WITHOUT YOU LORD, WE COULD NOT STAND
WE NEED YOUR LOVE, REACH OUT YOUR HAND
OH GLORIOUS KING WHO DIED FOR ME
FROM ALL TEMPTATIONS, SET US FREE
FOR YOU ARE GOD, THE ONLY ONE
FATHER, HOLY SPIRIT AND BLESSED SON
LET US SPREAD YOUR GLORIOUS LIGHT
TO THOSE WHO STUMBLE IN THE DARK NIGHT

FROM PRIDE AND PREJUDICE SET US FREE
LET US ONLY LIVE FOR THEE
AND WHAT YOU HAVE TAUGHT IN YOUR HOLY WORD
WHEN WE ARE TROUBLED, AND OUR THOUGHTS ARE BLURRED
WE MUST REMEMBER, WE MUST RECALL
THAT PRIDE GOETH BEFORE A FALL
LORD, SHIELD US, YOUR CHILDREN, NEATH YOUR WINGS
WITH FAITH AND HOPE, YOUR PRAISES WE SING

MY DEAREST ONES

BEHOLD MY CHILDREN, I HAVE COME TONIGHT
TO GIVE YOU WHATSOEVER YOU MAY ASK OF ME
AND TO SPEAK OF MY SERVANTS WHO WALK IN THE LIGHT
WHO BOLDLY FIGHT TO SET SOULS FREE
MY LITTLE ONE WHOM I SO DEARLY LOVE
SO FULL OF MY SPIRIT, SO FULL OF MY LIGHT
ON HER I SHALL POUR BLESSINGS FROM ABOVE
FOR SHE LOVES ME, HER LORD, WITH ALL OF HER MIGHT

HER SPOUSE, WHO SILENTLY WATCHES OVER ALL
MEEKLY, HE ANSWERED HIS SAVIOR'S CALL
TO SERVE OTHERS, TO FREE THEM IN MY HOLY NAME
WELL DONE, GOOD SERVANT, WE SHALL MEET AGAIN
AND THE GENTLE SON WHO SO GALLANTLY LEADS
MY CHILDREN TO WORSHIP, IN HIM I'M WELL PLEASED
IN MY NAME HE TRUSTS, AND OBEYS MY COMMANDS
AND FOR HIS LORD HE MAKES A STAND

AND THERE ARE AMONG YOU, OTHERS, WHO LOVE
TO WORK FOR THEIR LORD, FROM HEAVEN ABOVE
ONE WHO QUIETLY SPEAKS, AND SPREADS MY WORD TO ALL
THESE CHILDREN I TREASURE, THEY ANSWERED MY CALL
AND TO YOU, MY CHILDREN, WHOM I CALLED HERE TONIGHT
I LOVE YOU SO DEEPLY, IN YOU, I DELIGHT
AND TO THE ONE WHO OBEDIENTLY TAKES DOWN MY WORDS
OF MY UNDYING LOVE, MY CHILD, BE ASSURED

NOW, MY CHILDREN, I MUST TELL YOU HOW PLEASED I AM
IN THE PRAISES YOU SING, TO THE INNOCENT LAMB
FOR HE WHO IS IN THE MIDST OF THE GREAT THRONE
SHALL DELIGHT IN BRINGING HIS CHILDREN HOME
STILL, THERE IS MUCH MORE YOU MUST DO
AS YOU KNOW, I CONTINUE TO WORK THROUGH YOU
TO HEAL THE SICK, THE LOST AND THE LAME
THIS YOU SHALL CONTINUE TO DO IN MY NAME

FOR I GAVE YOU MY SPIRIT WITH ALL OF HIS POWER
TO SAVE MANY SOULS, FOR YOU KNOW NOT THE HOUR
WHEN, I, THE LORD, SHALL RETURN AT LAST
WHEN THE HEAVENS SHALL OPEN WITH A TRUMPET BLAST
FEAR NOT, MY CHILDREN, FOR THE LORD IS WITH THEE
ON MY RETURN, MY LITTLE ONES, YOU SHALL BE
WITH THE FATHER, THE SPIRIT, THE BLESSED SON
FOR I LOVE YOU FOREVER, MY DEAREST ONES

ONLY YOU, LORD

ONLY YOU LORD, ARE MY SALVATION, MY HOPE, MY TRUST, MY LOVE
I AM NOTHING WITHOUT YOU LORD, LET YOUR GRACE FLOW FROM ABOVE
WITHOUT IT I AM HELPLESS, LET IT NOT BE TAKEN FROM ME
IN YOUR HANDS I PLACE MY SOUL, TO YOUR OPEN ARMS I FLEE
ONLY YOU LORD, CAN SAVE ME, I AM POWERLESS ON MY OWN
I NEED ONLY YOU LORD, TO SHOW ME THE WAY HOME
I AM YOUR CREATION, YOU KNEW ME BEFORE MY BEING
YOU BREATHED YOUR SPIRIT WITHIN ME, YOU ARE MY LORD SUPREME

ONLY YOUR PRECIOUS BLOOD, LORD, CAN SAVE ME FROM ETERNAL DEATH
IT IS ONLY YOU, MY SAVIOR, WITHOUT YOU I HAVE NO BREATH
I CAN NOT SLEEP, NOR PRAY, NOR RISE WITHOUT YOUR MIGHTY HAND
AGAINST THE CUNNING ENEMY, THROUGH YOU, LORD, I WILL STAND
ONLY THE GIFT OF HOLY FEAR, CAN SAVE MY WRETCHED SOUL
FOR WITH IT COMES YOUR WISDOM, TO HELP ME REACH MY GOAL
AND WHEN YOU CALL ME LORD, HELP ME REACH YOUR HEAVENLY THRONE
MERCIFUL, HOLY SAVIOR, ONLY YOU CAN TAKE ME HOME

ONLY YOU, LORD, AND YOUR TENDER MERCY, CAN GUIDE ME ON THE PATH
YOUR PATIENT LOVE AND FORGIVENESS, CAN SAVE ME FROM THE WRATH
TO ONLY YOU, LORD, I SHALL TURN, I PLACE MY HOPE IN THEE
YOUR PRECIOUS BLOOD, WAS SHED FOR ALL, IN YOUR BOUNTIFUL MERCY
THERE IS NO WAY THAT I CAN EARN MY PLACE IN PARADISE
YOUR LIFE, DEATH AND RESURRECTION HAS PAID THE RANSOM PRICE
OH JESUS, I ASK IN YOUR HOLY NAME, I COME ON BENDED KNEE
FOR ONLY YOU LORD, CAN HEAL ME, ONLY YOU CAN SET ME FREE

RETURN TO ME, MY CHILDREN

RETURN TO ME MY CHILDREN, I AM WAITING HERE FOR YOU
MY ARMS ARE OPEN WIDE AND MY SACRED HEART IS TOO
THIS IS THE TIME FOR TURNING YOUR HEART UNTO YOUR LORD
THE TIME FOR YOU TO RECONCILE WITH THE GOD WHOM YOU ADORE
TOGETHER WE SHALL RECALL MY DEATH ON THE CROSS
THAT IS WHERE I GAVE MY LIFE FOR MY CHILDREN, WHO WERE LOST
WHATEVER I, YOUR LORD, MUST DO TO SAVE MY CHILDREN THAT I LOVE SO
WILLINGLY AND WITHOUT A CRY TO MY DEATH AGAIN, I WOULD GO
BUT KNOW THAT I AM YOUR GOD, THE CHRIST
PERFECT SACRIFICE NEED NOT BE OFFERED TWICE
FOR THE RANSOM WAS PAID, NOT WITH MONEY
BUT WITH YOUR LIVING GOD'S OWN LIFE
AS IT WAS FORETOLD AND AS IT WAS ORDAINED FROM ALL ETERNITY
I, THE SON, WOULD BEAR THE BLAME AND SET THE CAPTIVES FREE
AND SO I DIED, UPON THE CROSS, BUT TRIUMPHANTLY, I DID RISE
FEAR NOT, MY CHILDREN, COME WITH HASTE; YOUR SAVIOR IS TRULY ALIVE
MY CHILDREN, PLACE YOUR HOPE IN ME TODAY
BEHOLD, MY LITTLE ONES, I HAVE SHOWN THE WAY
YOU SHALL SHARE MY GLORY; COME LITTLE ONES, ARISE
AND YOU SHALL SHARE IN MY RESURRECTION
WHICH LEADS STRAIGHT TO PARADISE
WHERE THERE IS NO PUNISHMENT, NO RETRIBUTION
WHERE THERE IS NO SEPARATION, AND NO PAIN
BUT THE TREASURES OF HEAVEN, YOU SHALL GAIN
THERE SHALL BE NO TEARS FLOWING FROM YOUR EYES,
JUST ETERNAL JOY, HAPPINESS, PEACE, AND NO GOODBYES

PRECIOUS BLOOD

OH GOOD JESUS, PRECIOUS SAVIOR, WE PROCLAIM
WE BOW OUR HEADS AT YOUR SACRED NAME
YOU ARE OUR SAVIOR, WHO DIED ON THE CROSS
FOR OUR WRETCHED SOULS, YOU PAID THE COST
YOU CAME TO THIS WORLD, AS AN INNOCENT BUD
AND TO SAVE THE WORLD, SHED YOUR SACRED BLOOD
IT WAS NOT FOR THE RIGHTEOUS, LORD, THAT YOU CAME
BUT FOR UNFORTUNATE SINNERS, YOU BORE THE BLAME
SINNERS NOT WORTHY TO LOOK UPON YOUR FACE
NEVERTHELESS, LORD, YOU TOOK OUR PLACE
WE WERE NOT WORTHY TO CRAWL THROUGH THE MIRE AND MUD
BUT NOW WE ARE COVERED BY YOUR PRECIOUS BLOOD

OH LORD HOW CAN WE EVER THANK YOU ENOUGH
WE, WHO CALL ON YOU, LORD, WHEN TIMES ARE TOUGH
AND SOMETIMES FORGET TO THANK YOU, OUR GOD
AS THROUGH THIS LIFE, WE CARELESSLY PLOD
NEVER GIVING A THOUGHT TO OUR SAVING LORD
WHO DESERVES TO BE WORSHIPPED AND ADORED
BUT WE ARE MINDFUL NOW, LORD; WE ARE HERE TONIGHT
TO SING YOUR PRAISE AND TO JOIN IN THE FIGHT
TO WORK IN THE VINEYARD; MAKE YOUR MESSAGE HEARD
TO ALL WHO WILL LISTEN, WE SHALL DECLARE YOUR WORD
WE WERE NOT WORTHY TO CRAWL THROUGH THE MIRE AND MUD
BUT NOW WE ARE COVERED BY YOUR PRECIOUS BLOOD

OH PRECIOUS LORD WHO HAS SET ME FREE
I THANK YOU FOR ALL YOU HAVE DONE FOR ME
YOUR PATIENCE AND KINDNESS, I SHALL NOT FORGET
I AM NOT WORTHY, THIS I KNOW, AND YET
YOUR FORGIVENESS AND MERCY HAVE NO END
ONLY SON OF THE FATHER, HIS FLOCK YOU DO TEND
FOR US YOU CAME, YOU DIED AND ROSE TO GLORY
YOUR EARTHLY LIFE IS A WELL KNOWN STORY
TRIUMPHANT FOREVER, OVER SIN AND DEATH
YOU RANSOMED YOUR CHILDREN WITH YOUR DYING BREATH
WE WERE NOT WORTHY TO CRAWL THROUGH THE MIRE AND MUD
BUT NOW WE ARE COVERED BY YOUR PRECIOUS BLOOD

PEACE OF THE LORD

OH PRECIOUS LORD OF DIVINE LOVE AND PEACE
I ASK YOU NOW, MY GOD, TO EXTEND THY SACRED HANDS
UNTO THY HUMBLE SERVANT, WHO CRIES UNTO THEE
FOR MERCY AND COMPASSION AS I TRY TO UNDERSTAND
THE CONFUSION AND ELATION OF WHAT
HAS COME TO PASS IN THESE LAST FEW HOURS
THROUGH YOUR HOLY SPIRIT AND YOUR SERVANTS
YOU DEMONSTRATED YOUR MIGHTY POWERS
AS YOU COMMANDED BEFORE YOUR ASSENCION ON THAT DAY
THEY PRAYED TO THE FATHER, FOR OUR SISTER, EARNESTLY
AND IN THE HOLY NAME OF JESUS, THEY CAST HER PAIN AWAY
HER HEARING WAS RESTORED, ALLELUIA, PRAISE TO THEE

FOR FROM THY VERY MOUTH, MY LORD, I HAVE HEARD
THEE SAY, "ASK AND IT SHALL BE GIVEN UNTO THEE"
BEHOLD, MY GOD, I HUMBLY ASK IN THY HOLY NAME
OH HOLY, BLESSED SAVIOR, LAMB OF GOD, SET ME FREE
FROM PHYSICAL ILLNESS, FROM PAST HURTS
FROM UNFORGIVENESS THAT KEEPS ME BOUND
FROM ALL ANGER AND RESENTMENT IN MY HEART
LORD I PRAY, HELP ME CAST THEM DOWN
TO THE FOOT OF YOUR CROSS ON WHICH YOU, MY SAVIOR, DIED
HELP ME CAST AWAY THE PAIN THAT HAUNTS ME
HURTFUL MEMORIES, IN YOUR HOLY WOUNDS LET THEM HIDE
FROM ALL THOSE THINGS, OH GRACIOUS LORD, SET ME FREE

I REMEMBER THY WORDS, OH GOD, "SEEK AND YE SHALL FIND'
BEHOLD, I SEEK THY UNDERSTANDING
MERCIFUL SAVIOR, GRANT IT UNTO ME
FOR, MY PRECIOUS JESUS, ONLY YOU CAN SET ME FREE
LORD YOU SAID, "KNOCK AND THE DOOR SHALL BE OPENED'
BEHOLD, I KNOCK, LORD, BID ME TO COME IN
KEEP ME SAFE FROM THE CUNNING ENEMY
AND LET HIM NOT ENTICE ME TO SIN
LORD, FROM ALL PAIN AND ILLNESS, I BEG, GIVE ME RELEASE,
I PRAY THEE, LORD, ALSO, THAT YOU WILL GRANT ME PEACE
MAY I, WHEN MY DAYS ARE OVER, COME, LAMB OF GOD, TO THEE
JESUS, IN YOUR LOVING MERCY, DO NOT ABANDON ME

SPIRITS OF GOD

MY BELOVED CHILDREN, I BESEECH YOU TO MAKE YOURSELVES
FAMILIAR WITH THESE SAVING WORDS
THAT MY SERVANT, JOHN, WROTE FOR THE WORLD TO OBSERVE
PAY STRICT ATTENTION, MY CHILDREN, IT IS ALSO A WARNING FOR YOU
THESE ARE THE WORDS OF GOD WHO CAN NOT SPEAK WHAT IS UNTRUE
"DEARLY BELOVED, BELIEVE NOT IN EVERY SPIRIT,
BUT TRY THE SPIRITS WHETHER THEY BE OF GOD AND THE CHRISTIAN FAITH
FOR MANY ARE THE FALSE PROPHETS OUT TO DESTROY; THEY LIE IN WAIT
"BY THIS IS THE SPIRIT OF GOD KNOWN;
EVERY SPIRIT WHO HAS CONFESSED YOUR LORD JESUS CHRIST
TO HAVE COME INTO THE FLESH, IS OF GOD:
AND EVERY SPIRIT, THAT DISSOLVED JESUS"
BEWARE, FOR SUCH A SPIRIT IS NOT OF GOD
"THIS IS ANTICHRIST OF WHOM YOU HAVE HEARD
HE THAT COMETH, AND HE IS NOW ALREADY IN THE WORLD",
TAKE HEED CHILDREN; HEAR THESE WORDS; BE NOT DIM
"YOU ARE OF GOD" LITTLE CHILDREN AND "YOU HAVE OVERCOME HIM"
TO YOUR LORD, EACH ONE OF YOU IS LIKE A PRECIOUS PEARL
"BECAUSE GREATER IS HE THAT IS IN YOU, MY LITTLE ONES,
THAN HE THAT IS IN THE WORLD"
"THEY ARE OF THIS WORLD, THEREFORE OF THE WORLD THEY SPEAK
HE THAT KNOWETH GOD HEARETH THEE,
HE THAT IS NOT OF GOD, HEARETH THEE NOT"
MY CHILDREN, BE WARY OF THE EVIL ONE WHO ROAMS THE WORLD
WHO WILL STEAL SOULS BY LIES AND DECEIT
HE ENTICES MANY SOULS TO LOVE
ONLY THE THINGS OF THE WORLD
SO MANY FALL BY HIS EVIL WAYS AND MEET DEFEAT
"FOR THEIR WAYS ARE NOT OF GOD",
THEIRS ARE THE WAYS OF RUINATION, DAMNATION AND TERROR
"BY THIS WE KNOW, BELOVED, THE SPIRIT OF TRUTH,
AND THE SPIRIT OF ERROR"
SO PRAISE THE HOLY ONE, KEEP GOING DEEPER INTO MY HOLY SPIRIT
SALVATION IS YOURS, TAKE YOUR FAITH TO THE WORLD AND SHARE IT

OH GOD, IN YOU ALONE

OH GOD, IN YOU ALONE, CAN I FIND PEACE
IN YOU ALONE, CAN I FIND LOVE
FOR YOUR PEACE AND LOVE ARE EVERLASTING
YOUR WONDERFUL BLESSINGS FAR SURPASSING
ANYTHING THE WORLD CAN GIVE
FOR YOU ALONE, MY GOD, I SHALL LIVE
ON THE PALM OF YOUR MIGHTY HAND
MY GOD, YOU HAVE GRACIOUSLY WRITTEN MY NAME
AND FOR THE SAKE OF MY SINFUL SOUL
YOUR ONLY SON, JESUS, BORE THE BLAME
FOR ME HE DIED, FOR ME HE ROSE
AND FOR ME HE SHALL EVER LIVE
I SING HOLY, HOLY, HOLY LORD
TO MY GOD WHO LONGS TO FORGIVE

JESUS BORE THE HEAVY WOODEN CROSS
MADE HEAVIER BY MY SINS
SO THAT HEAVEN'S DOOR WOULD BE OPENED
AND THAT, I, YOUR CHILD, MAY ENTER IN
WHEN MY LIFE ON THIS EARTH IS THROUGH
I SHALL GO BY YOUR HOLY GRACE
YOU SHALL LOOK UPON ME WITH MERCY
AND SEE YOUR SON, MY SAVIOR'S FACE
HIS LIFE, DEATH AND RESURRECTION
HAS SET HIS LOST CHILDREN FREE
AND TO HELP US YOU SEND THE COMFORTER
OH HOLY SPIRIT EVER STAY BY ME
YOU, WHO GO FORTH FROM THE FATHER AND FROM THE SON,
HOLY, HOLY, POWERFUL GOD, HOLY IMMORTAL ONE

MY LORD JESUS, HOLY IS YOUR NAME

THERE IS A STORY OLD, AND IT IS OFTEN TOLD
ABOUT THE SON OF GOD, WHO DIED ON CALVARY
HE CAME TO EARTH BY A VIRGIN BIRTH
A BABE, WHO WAS LONG AGO FORETOLD
A PRECIOUS CHILD, SON OF GOD AND MAN
WHO IS THERE ON EARTH WHO CAN UNDERSTAND
HOW THIS THING COULD EVER COME TO BE
THAT YOU, OH GOD, WOULD COME TO SET US FREE

OH INFINITE MERCY, HOW YOU LOVE US ALL
YOU MADE US YOUR CHILDREN, BY OUR NAMES YOU WILL CALL
IN SPITE OF OUR WEAKNESS, IN SPITE OF OUR SINS
YOU OPENED YOUR HEART AND BID US TO COME IN
OH HOW CAN WE THANK YOU, FOR YOUR ETERNAL LOVE
THERE IS NO ANSWER ON EARTH, OR HEAVEN ABOVE
THOUGH WE ARE UNDESERVING, YOU SENT YOUR ONLY SON
FOR OUR SINFUL WAYS, YOU GAVE YOUR CHOSEN ONE

THIS DAY, TO YOU, MY LORD, I SURRENDER MY ALL
BUT FOR YOUR TENDER MERCIES, ETERNAL DEATH WOULD CALL
I WILL SING OF YOU, MY SAVIOR, UNTIL THE DAY I DIE
AND WHEN YOU CALL ME LORD, LET ME COME TO YOUR SIDE
YOU CAME FOR THE AFFLICTED, YOU CAME FOR THE POOR
YOU CAME NOT FOR THE RIGHTEOUS, BUT YOU OPENED THE DOOR
TO THE SICK, THE LONELY, THE BLIND AND THE LAME
OH THANK YOU BLESSED JESUS, MOST HOLY IS YOUR NAME

I BOW MY HEAD IN PRAYER, AND KNOW THAT YOU ARE THERE
ALWAYS WAITING, AND ALWAYS LISTENING TO MY PLEAS
OH LORD OF RIGHTEOUSNESS, HOW CAN THIS BE
THE KING OF THE WORLD, YOU CAME TO SET US FREE
FOR YOU ARE WITHOUT BLEMISH, YOU ARE WITHOUT BLAME
YOU ARE STRONG, YET GENTLE AS YOU SOFTLY CALL MY NAME
IN YOU, BE ALL GLORY, FILL OUR HEARTS WITH GLAD REFRAIN
WE SING HOLY, HOLY, HOLY IS YOUR NAME

MY CHILDREN, HOW PLEASED I AM

MY LITTLE ONES, HOW PLEASED I AM WITH YOU
FOR THE SAKE OF MY HOLY NAME, YOU HAVE MUCH TO DO
YOU HAVE CONCENTED TO RECEIVE A SPECIAL INDWELLING
OF MY HOLY SPIRIT, NOW YOU SHALL BE TELLING
ALL THAT YOU MEET, ABOUT YOUR SAVING LORD
WHO MUST, ABOVE ALL THINGS, BE WORSHIPPED AND ADORED
WITH YOUR HEARTS AND MINDS ON THE HOLY, PERFECT ONE
YOU SHALL BE FOLLOWERS OF MY BELOVED SON

MY HOLY SPIRIT, MY POWER IN THIS WORLD
SHALL LEAD YOU FORWARD WITH WINGS UNFURLED
YOU SHALL CALL ON ME, THROUGH MY PRECIOUS SON
FOR IN HIS HOLY NAME, MUCH WILL BE DONE
SO MY BELOVED ONES, YOU MUST FERVENTLY PRAY
THAT THE HOLY SPIRIT SHOWS YOU THE WAY
ASK FOR THE GIFTS, THERE ARE SEVEN PLUS TWO
THAT MY HOLY SPIRIT MAY BESTOW ON YOU

GREAT IS THE HARVEST, BUT THE WORKERS ARE FEW
YOU HAVE BEEN CHOSEN, GOD SHALL WORK THROUGH YOU
IF YOU ARE WEAKENED BY THE VASTNESS OF THIS FIGHT
TURN TO YOUR SAVIOR; HE IS THE ONE TRUE LIGHT
NOW WHATSOEVER YOU SHALL ASK IN HIS NAME
I SHALL NOT REFUSE, FOR HE TOOK THE BLAME
HE RANSOMED MY CHILDREN, IN THEIR FEARFUL PLIGHT
THE SON IS THE WAY, IS THE TRUTH AND IS THE LIFE

MY BELOVED, YOU MUST FOLLOW THE LEAD
OF THE HOLY SPIRIT, WHO IS GOD INDEED
FOR WE ARE THE TRINITY, YET, WE ARE ONE
HOLY THE FATHER, HOLY THE SPIRIT, HOLY THE SON
YOUR REWARD SHALL BE THAT WHICH YOU CAN NOT BUY
PEACE, LOVE AND FORGIVENESS, FOR WHICH HE DIED
OBEY ME, THE FATHER, AND FOLLOW THE SON
TRUST IN THE COMFORTER, MY WILL SHALL BE DONE

I THANK YOU LORD

I THANK YOU LORD FOR GIVING ME LIFE
I THANK YOU LORD, YOU BROUGHT ME THROUGH STRIFE
I THANK YOU LORD, FOR YOUR ABOUNDING LOVE
I THANK YOU LORD FOR YOUR GRACE FROM ABOVE
YOU WERE THERE. LORD. ON THE DAY I WAS BORN
YOU WERE THERE WITH ME WHEN I FELT TORN
THERE WITH THE ANGELS YOU ASSIGNED TO ME
WHEN I FELT THAT GOOD THINGS COULD NEVER BE

YOUR HOLY PRESENCE WAS THERE WITH ME
WHEN I LEARNED TO PRAY AT MY DEAR MOTHER'S KNEE
AND WHEN I WAS FRIGHTENED AND HURT AND CONFUSED
WHEN LOVED ONES HURT ME, YOU CARRIED ME THROUGH
I THANK YOU LORD FOR THE BLESSINGS YOU POURED
WHILE IN HUMBLE WORSHIP, I THEE, ADORED
I THANK YOU FOR THE SPIRIT THAT YOU BREATHED INTO ME
I THANK YOU LORD FOR SETTNG ME FREE

MY LIFE, THOUGH NOT PERFECT, I OFFER TO THEE
I THANK YOU FOR TAKING YOUR TIME FOR ME
AND WHEN I WAS LIVING IN DEEP DESPAIR
YOU LIFTED ME UP, YOU WERE ALWAYS THERE
YOU HAVE BROUGHT ME THROUGH DARKNESS
YOU HAVE BROUGHT ME THROUGH PAIN
YOU GIVE ME FORGIVENESS AGAIN AND AGAIN
LORD, I THANK YOU FOR THE GIFTS THAT YOU GIVE
I THANK YOU, LORD, FOR DYING SO THAT I MIGHT LIVE

THE WORD

MY BELOVED CHILDREN, IT IS WRITTEN IN MY HOLY WORD
THAT YOU MUST LOVE YOUR GOD WITH ALL YOUR HEART AND SOUL
FOR IT IS I WHO CREATED YOU AND ALL THAT IS SEEN AND HEARD
GOD HAS GIVEN YOU ALL YOU NEED TO LIVE, TO BE WHOLE
IT IS WRITTEN ALSO THAT AS, I, YOUR GOD, AM HOLY, SO YOU MUST BE
IT IS WHY I CAME TO EARTH, TO SET MY CHILDREN FREE
DO UNTO OTHERS AS YOU WOULD HAVE THEM DO UNTO YOU
TO SAVE YOUR IMMORTAL SOULS YOU MUST, TO YOUR GOD, BE TRUE

LIVE IN THE LIGHT OF YOUR SAVIOR WHO DESCENDED FROM ABOVE
I CAME TO SAVE MY CHILDREN, YOU, WHOM I DEARLY LOVE
BE GOOD UNTO YOUR NEIGHBOR, IF HE BE NEEDY, YOU MUST GIVE
BE THERE FOR THE LOST AND LONELY, AND FOREVER YOU SHALL LIVE
YOU MUST DO NO HARM TO OTHERS, IN WORD, IN THOUGHT, OR IN DEED
PAY HEED TO THE DOWN TRODDEN, IF YOU CAN, FULFILL THEIR NEED
KEEP WATCH THAT YOU DO NOT OFFEND YOUR GOD, THE ONE TRUE LIGHT
STEP CAREFULLY, IN ALL YOU DO, TO REMAIN HOLY IN MY SIGHT

HOWEVER, I AM REMEMBERING THE COVENANT I HAVE WITH THEE
THE COVENANT OF MY PRECIOUS BLOOD THAT SETS MY CHILDREN FREE
FOR I KNOW YOU ARE MERE MORTALS, AND THAT SOMETIMES YOU MAY FALL
THAT IS WHY I GAVE MY LIFE, THE GREATEST GIFT OF ALL
BE KIND EVEN UNTO YOUR ENEMIES, OFFER THEM THE PEACE I GIVE
FOR I DIED FOR THEM ALSO, AND I AM RISEN AND FOREVER I LIVE
BEHOLD YOU SHALL HAVE ALL THAT I PROMISED, YES, AND MUCH MORE
FOR I AM THE WORD COME DOWN FROM HEAVEN, THE SAVIOR YOU ADORE

PRAYER TO OUR HEAVENLY FATHER

OH GOD OUR FATHER, GOD OF ALL MANKIND
WE GIVE YOU ALL GLORY, WE GIVE YOU ALL PRAISE
YOU ARE OUR FATHER ETERNAL, ALMIGHTY, AND YET SO KIND
YOU GIVE US ABUNDANT LOVE, AND WE LOVE YOUR HOLY WAYS
YOU SHOWED YOUR CHILDREN THE WAY AND GAVE US THE BREAD OF LIFE
HIS SAVING LOVE IS ENDURING; HE WALKS WITH US THROUGH STRIFE
THROUGH THE POWER OF THE HOLY SPIRIT, YOUR SON CAME TO US
HE IS YOUR ONLY BEGOTTEN SON, OUR REDEEMER, OUR LORD JESUS

HE WILLINGLY GAVE HIS LIFE TO SAVE OUR WRETCHED SOULS
OBEDIENT TO YOU, HIS FATHER, REVEALED BY YOUR PROPHETS OF OLD,
AND WHEN OUR LORD, OUR SAVIOR, FINISHED HIS TIME ON EARTH,
HE GAVE US HIS PRECIOUS MOTHER, TO HELP US WIN OUR WORTH
NOT ONLY DID HE DIE FOR US, TO TAKE AWAY OUR SINS
HE SENT US THE HOLY SPIRIT WHO NOW DWELLS WITHIN
HEAVENLY FATHER, WE PROCLAIM AND SING OF YOUR DIVINITY
HOLY, HOLY, HOLY GOD, BLESSED TRINITY

AMEN

THE CUP, MY FATHER GAVE TO ME

MY CHILDREN, THE CUP WHICH MY FATHER GAVE TO ME
I ACCEPTED GLADLY AND I DRANK THEREOF
TO OBEY MY FATHER'S HOLY WILL
AND TO PORTRAY HIS ETERNAL LOVE
FOR THERE WAS A PURPOSE TO THE FATHER'S DIVINE PLAN
THE SON OF GOD WOULD ALSO BECOME THE SON OF MAN
FOR GOD WOULD NOT FORSAKE HIS CHILDREN
NEITHER WOULD HE CAST THEM AWAY
FOR HE IS OUR SAVING LORD,
YESTERDAY, TOMORROW AND TODAY

IT IS THE LORD, LET HIM DO WHAT SEEMETH GOOD,
LET HIM DECIDE FOR HIS CHILDREN WHAT HE WOULD
FOR HE WOULD GIVE HIS BELOVED CHILDREN THE SAVING CUP
AND SO, HIS ONLY BEGOTTEN SON WOULD BE LIFTED UP
BE NOT AFRAID, LET YOUR HEARTS OPEN TO ME
FOR I AM THE MESSIAH, THE GOD WHO SETS YOU FREE
I SHALL GIVE YOU STRENGTH TO OVERCOME THE ENEMY
THEN, YOU SHALL LIFT UP YOUR VOICES AND YOU SHALL WORSHIP ME

SO, MY BELOVED CHILDREN, HARKEN NOW, UNTO ME
FOR I AM THE LORD YOUR GOD, FOR ALL ETERNITY
I SHALL NOT FORSAKE YOU, NOR CAUSE YOU TO HAVE FEAR
FOR YOU, MY FAITHFUL CHILDREN, I SHALL ALWAYS BE NEAR
BE ASSURED THAT MY MERCY AND MY LOVE HAVE NO BOUNDS
FOR YOU I WAS BORN, AND POURED MY BLOOD UPON THE GROUND
MY BELOVED LITTLE ONES, I LOVE YOU SO VERY DEEPLY
IT IS WHY I DRANK OF THE CUP WHICH MY FATHER GAVE TO ME

THE HOLY ONE

IF YOU, MY CHILDREN, DESIRE TO DWELL WITH YOUR LORD
WHEN THE DAYS OF YOUR EARTHLY LIFE ARE GONE
SPEND YOUR LIVES WISELY, AND THE ONE TRUE GOD, ADORE
PRAY CONSTANTLY FOR HIS HELP, PRAISE HIM FOREVERMORE
YOU MUST STRIVE TO BE LIKE JESUS, GOD'S ONLY BEGOTTEN SON
FOR ALL YOUR DAYS UPON THE EARTH, BE A TEMPLE OF THE HOLY ONE
LOVE YOUR LORD AND LOVE THY NEIGHBOR; A HOLY LIFE STRIVE TO LIVE
FOR YOUR GOD IS SLOW TO ANGER AND QUICK TO FORGIVE

YOUR GOD WILL NOT FAIL YOU, NOR WILL HE FORSAKE YOU
SO, MY CHILDREN, SEEK HIS HOLY FACE, CONTINUALLY
THERE IS NONE LIKE HIM IN ALL THE EARTH, PRESENT, FUTURE OR PAST
KNOW THAT I AM HE; I AM THE FIRST AND I AM ALSO THE LAST
LET MY WORDS DWELL IN YOUR HEART; OBEY THE PRECEPTS OF THE LORD
MY WORD IS QUICK AND POWERFUL, SHARPER THAN A TWO-EDGED SWORD
I AM YOUR GOD, NAME ABOVE ALL NAMES AND LORD OF ALL LORDS
I AM THE KING OF GLORY, THE MOST HIGH, ALWAYS ADORED

BE AWARE THAT YOUR GOD KNOWS THOSE WHO TRY THEIR BEST
TO IMITATE THEIR SAVIOR, AND THROUGH HIM THEY SHALL BE BLESSED
REMEMBER, EXCEPT A MAN BE BORN AGAIN OF FIRE AND THE SPIRIT,
HE SHALL NOT CLAIM ETERNAL BLISS, MY TREASURES, NOT INHEIRIT
HE'LL NOT ENTER INTO THE KINGDOM OF GOD, THE MOST HOLY ONE
YOU MUST BE BORN AGAIN IN THE SPIRIT, TO HAVE KINSHIP WITH THE SON
PRAY FOR A DEEP INDWELLING OF HIS SPIRIT, THE POWERFUL ONE
HOLY, HOLY, HOLY GOD ALMIGHTY, WHICH WAS AND IS, AND IS TO COME

OH LOVE DIVINE

OH LORD, OUR PRECIOUS SAVIOR
YOU CAME TO THIS WORLD OF SORROW
WE HAD NEED OF YOU, OH LOVE DIVINE
WITHOUT YOU, THERE WOULD BE NO TOMORROW
YOU LEAD US ON THE PATH OF RIGHTEOUSNESS
MAY OUR STEPS LEAD US STRAIGHT TO YOU
POUR YOUR GRACE UPON US, LORD
RESTORE US, MAKE OUR HEARTS ANEW

FOR YOU ARE JOY FAR SURPASSING
THE FOOLISH THINGS OF THIS WORLD
YOU ARE THE ONE TRUE GOD
OUR SAVIOR, WITH ARMS UNFURLED
TO HOLD US CLOSE TO YOUR SACRED HEART
OH GOD, NEVER LET US GO ASTRAY;
YOU ARE OUR LIVING GOD
SHOWING US THE WAY

YOU ARE LOVE EVERLASTING
OUR SAVIOR, OUR REDEEMER, OUR LORD
GOD'S ROYAL PRIEST, OF WHOM WE SING
THE JUST ONE, WHOM WE ADORE
AS A LITTLE BABE YOU CAME TO US
ON A DARK, COLD WINTER'S NIGHT
THE LONG AWAITED SAVIOR,
TO BRING US INTO THE LIGHT

OH VIRGIN OF VIRGINS, OUR MOTHER
THANK YOU FOR SAYING YES
YOU CARRIED THE HOLY ONE IN YOUR WOMB
TO BRING US TRUE HAPPINESS
THE TRUE LIVING WORD, PROPHESIED OF OLD
BY THE HOLY SPIRIT, CONCEIVED
OH MOTHER, EVER VIRGIN
IN YOUR SON, WE SHALL EVER BELIEVE

OH GOD, OUR LOVING FATHER
BY YOUR PROPHETS, IT WAS FORETOLD
HOW YOU WOULD SEND YOUR ONLY SON
FULFILLING THE PROMISE OF OLD
TO BRING US OUT OF THE DARKNESS
INTO HIS MOST HOLY LIGHT
THE KING OF KINGS, OH LOVE DIVINE
BORN ON THAT WINTERY NIGHT

COME, FOR ALL IS READY

MY CHILDREN, KNOW THAT MANY SOULS LOSE HOPE
AND MANY IN THE WORLD, LOSE FAITH
FOR THOSE WHO ARE NOT OF GOD; WHO WITH SATAN PLAYS
LORE MY CHILDREN INTO FOLLOWING THEIR EVIL WAYS
BUT YOU WHO REMAIN FAITHFUL, SHALL SEE MY HOLY FACE
UPON YOU, MY LITTLE ONES, I SHALL POUR DOWN MY GRACE
I SHALL SEND MY HOLY SPIRIT TO DWELL DEEPER IN YOUR SOULS
THIS, YOU WILL NEED, MY BELOVED, IF YOU ARE TO MEET YOUR GOALS

FOR YOU KNOW THAT I AM THE WAY, THE TRUTH AND THE LIFE
FOLLOW THE SON, THE LIVING GOD, AND WALK IN HIS HOLY LIGHT
I TELL YOU, KEEP ON ASKING, YOU WILL RECEIVE WHAT YOU ASK FOR
KEEP ON SEEKING AND YOU SHALL RECEIVE, THAT, AND EVEN MORE
KEEP KNOCKING AND YOU SHALL BEHOLD YOUR SAVIOR, WHO IS SO KIND
TRULY, EVERYONE WHO ASKS, RECEIVES; EVERYONE WHO SEEKS, FINDS
AND TO EVERYONE WHO KNOCKS, THE DOOR SHALL BE OPENED WIDE
LOOK TO ME, YOUR SAVING GOD, WHO STANDS ALWAYS AT YOUR SIDE

FOR I CAME, NOT INTO THE WORLD TO CONDEMN IT, BUT TO SAVE IT
I CAME NOT INTO THE WORLD, TO SEEK MY LIFE, BUT TO GIVE IT
I CAME IN OBEDIENCE TO MY FATHER, EVEN UNTO DEATH
YES, I RANSOMED MY BELOVED CHILDREN, WITH MY DYING BREATH
I LEFT MY GLORY, AND MY KINGDOM OF HEAVEN, SENT BY MY FATHER
I CAME TO BE, FOR MY CHILDREN, THE TRUE LIVING WATER
TO THOSE THAT SERVE, WHO ARE WILLING AND STEADY
I SHALL SAY, "MY LITTLE ONES, COME; FOR ALL IS READY"

THE EVIL ONE

THERE IS AN EVIL ENTITY IN THE WORLD, IT IS SAD TO SAY
BUT HAVE NO FEAR, MY CHILDREN, FOR OVER ME, HE HAS NO SWAY
FOR I AM THE LORD, YOUR GOD, FOREVER HOLY AM I
HE TRIUMPHS NOT, OVER YOUR LORD, NO MATTER HOW EVIL AND SLY
HE MEANS, BY EVIL DECEIT, TO STEAL MY CHILDREN'S SOULS
MY HOLY SPIRIT IS WITHIN YOU, HE SHALL NOT REACH HIS GOALS
MANY THE EVIL SOLDIERS, HE HAS IN HIS DOMAIN
BUT YOU SHALL CAST THEM OUT IN MY MOST HOLY NAME
MY CHILDREN, I AM SURE YOU KNOW OF WHOM I SPEAK
IT IS HE WHO TEMPTS AND DECEIVES, TO MAKE MY CHILDREN WEAK
HE HAS MANY SOLDIERS, BUT AGAINST ME THEY CAN NOT STAND
I AM THE ONLY SON OF GOD, THEY MUST OBEY MY COMMANDS

MY SAINTS AND MY ANGELS ARE EVER READY TO HEED
THE WILL OF THEIR ONE TRUE GOD, WHO FILLS THEIR EVERY NEED
THEY SHALL RIDE WITH THEIR LORD, WHO UPON HIS MIGHTY STEED
SHALL BANISH SATAN FROM THIS WORLD, AND SET THE CAPTIVES FREE
MY CHILDREN, DO NOT FEAR, BE NOT DISMAYED OR ALARMED
I SHALL RECLAIM MY KINGDOM, YOU SHALL NOT BE HARMED
DID NOT, I, YOUR LORD, COME DOWN FROM MY GLORY ON HIGH
DID I NOT CARRY THE HEAVY CROSS, ON WHICH I WAS TO DIE
FEAR NOT, MY BELOVED CHILDREN, YOUR LORD IS BY YOUR SIDE
I AM THE WAY, THE TRUTH, THE LIFE, LET MY SPIRIT BE YOUR GUIDE
MY BELOVED, I WANT TO GIVE YOU LIFE FOR EVERMORE
FOLLOW MY WAYS, AND YOU SHALL BE WITH THE SAVIOR YOU ADORE

HEED NOT THE TEMPTOR'S DECEPTIONS, FOR EVIL ARE HIS WAYS
AND HIS WAY IS RUIN AND DAMNATION, FOR THOSE WHO GO ASTRAY
MY COVENANT WITH MY CHILDREN, IS TRUE AND EVERLASTING
MY POWER AND MY MIGHT SHALL WIN, FOR IT IS FAR SURPASSING
ANY POWER IN THE NETHER WORLD, FOR I AM THE HOLY ONE
GOOD SHALL TRIUMPH OVER EVIL, GOD'S HOLY WILL BE DONE
PAY HEED TO YOUR SAVING LORD, STRIVE TO RESIST ALL SIN
AND BY THE TEMPTOR'S EVIL LIES, YOU SHALL NOT BE TAKEN IN
BUT KNOW THAT THOUGH YOU MAY SOMETIMES FALL
INTO SIN AGAINST YOUR SAVING LORD
CONFESS YOUR SINS, WITH SINCERITY AND SORROW
AND FORGIVENESS, MY CHILDREN, SHALL BE YOURS

THIS IS THE TIME

THIS IS THE TIME, THIS IS THE PLACE
THE HERE AND THE NOW FOR THE WHOLE HUMAN RACE
IF YOU WANT TO BE HAPPY, IF YOU WANT TO BE FREE
WALK OUT OF THE DARKNESS, AND COME FOLLOW ME
FOR YOU I CAME DOWN FROM HEAVEN ABOVE
TO TEACH YOU KINDNESS, TO TEACH YOU TO LOVE
IT WAS FOR YOU I WAS BORN, FOR YOU THAT I DIED
AND FOR YOU I AM RISEN, AND I AM ALIVE
LISTEN MY CHILDREN, HARKEN TO ME
I LOVE YOU SO DEEPLY, FOR ETERNITY

I AM HERE WAITING FOR YOU, COME WALK IN THE LIGHT
FOR I AM THE WAY, THE TRUTH AND THE LIFE
THE LIFE GIVING WATER, YOUR SAVIOR, YOUR LORD
THE TRUE LIVING BREAD, THE DOUBLE EDGED SWORD
I WANT TO TAKE AWAY YOUR HEARTS MADE OF STONE
AND GIVE YOU A NEW ONE, TO MAKE YOU MY OWN
I WANT NOT TO JUDGE YOU, WHEN THE END TIME COMES
I WANT TO WELCOME YOU AS MY DAUGHTERS, MY SONS
FOR YOU ARE MY CHILDREN, FOR ETERNITY
I LIVED, DIED, AND ROSE AGAIN TO SET YOUR SOULS FREE

THERE IS NO GREATER POWER, ABOVE OR BELOW
THERE IS NO GREATER LOVE, TO HAVE OR TO HOLD
I HAVE BEEN LIFTED UP FOR THE WHOLE WORLD TO SEE
AS I OBEYED MY FATHER, YOU MUST OBEY ME
SO GIVE ME ALL GLORY, AND WITH YOUR HANDS RAISED
WORSHIP YOUR SAVIOR, TO HIM BE ALL PRAISE
LIFT UP YOUR VOICES, AND SING TO YOUR LORD
FATHER, SON AND HOLY SPIRIT, ONE GOD ADORED

THE GREATEST GIFT

MY BROTHERS AND MY SISTERS, HEAR
THE LORD, OUR GOD, HAS SOMETHING TO SAY
HE WISHES TO REMIND HIS CHILDREN
WHAT WE SHOULD BE AWARE OF EVERY DAY
YOUR GOD AND MINE, WHO REIGNS OVER US ALL
WANTS US TO HEAR HIS PRECIOUS SON'S CALL
HE CAME TO US AS OUR REDEEMING LORD
SON OF GOD, THE GREATEST GIFT OF ALL

THIS GIFT OF GOD, HIS PRECIOUS SON
BECAME FLESH TO LIVE AMONG MANKIND
HE CAME TO SAVE OUR WRETCHED SOULS
TO HEAL THE SICK, THE LAME, THE BLIND
HE TAUGHT US HOW TO LIVE OUR LIVES
BY EXAMPLE, FROM THE WORD MADE FLESH
TO ALWAYS BE PLEASING TO OUR LORD
THEN WE SHALL HAVE TRUE HAPPINESS

MY BROTHERS AND MY SISTERS
WILL YOU CALL ON HIM TODAY
TO CLAIM HIM AS YOUR SAVIOR,
WALK IN HIS HOLY WAYS
ASK HIM FOR FORGIVENESS
FOR WE ARE SINFUL ONES
AND THANK HIM FOR HIS HOLY GIFTS
UNTIL HIS KINGDOM COME

WHEN HIS WORK ON EARTH WAS DONE
ON A CROSS HE WAS LIFTED HIGH
WILLINGLY HE GAVE HIS LIFE
YES, WILLINGLY HE DIED
HE SUFFERED ALL, TOOK ON OUR SINS
THE BLAMELESS ONE, WHO COULD NOT FALL
OUT OF GRACE, FOR HE IS GOD
THE GREATEST GIFT OF ALL

THE HOLY SPIRIT

THE HOLY SPIRIT, MY SISTERS AND BROTHERS,
IS A PERSON, NOT A FORCE OR A THNG OR A POWER
NOR AN IMPERSONAL FORCE LIKE MAGNETISM OR GRAVITY
NOR LIKE SOME MADE UP HERO OF THE HOUR
THE HOLY SPIRIT IS GOD, AS ARE THE FATHER AND THE SON
PART OF THE BLESSED TRINITY, YET, THEY ARE ONE
HE IS AND ALWAYS WAS, THE ONE WHO SANCTIFIES,
TEACHES AND INSTRUCTS, ILLUMINATES AND GUIDES
HE IS THE HELPER, THE CONSOLER, THE EDUCATOR
BAPTIZED IN THE SPIRIT NOW, YOU MUST ASK HIM FOR
THE GIFTS HE BESTOWS ON SERVANTS OF THE HOLY ONE
SO YOU MAY SERVE YOUR GOD; THAT HIS WILL MAY BE DONE

NOW THESE ARE THE GIFTS THAT HE BESTOWS ON THOSE WHO SERVE
NOT EVERYONE WILL RECEIVE ALL, AS IS WRITTEN IN HIS WORD
WORD OF WISDOM, WORD OF KNOWLEDGE, THE DISCERNING OF THE SPIRITS
GIFTS OF HEALING, THE WORKING OF MIRACLES, LET ALL WITH EARS HEAR IT
CHARISMA OF FAITH, PROPHECY, GIFTS OF TONGUES OF VARIOUS KINDS
INTERPRETATION OF TONGUES, OH LET HIS SPIRIT FILL OUR MINDS
THESE ARE THE GIFTS OF THE HOLY SPIRIT FOR THOSE WHO BELIEVE
WISDOM, UNDERSTANDING, COUNSEL, FORTITUDE, KNOWLEDGE, PIETY
AS WELL AS THIS ONE, "FEAR THE LORD YOUR GOD", WHO SETS US FREE
FOR HE IS ALL POWERFUL, ALL KNOWING, ALL LOVING AND ALMIGHTY
THESE ARE THE SIGNS OF THOSE REBORN OF THE SPIRIT OF THE SON OF MAN
IN HIS HOLY NAME, THEY SHALL HEAL THE SICK BY THE LAYING OF HANDS

AND THEY SHALL CAST OUT DEMONS AND SPEAK WITH NEW TONGUES
THEY SHALL RAISE THEIR HANDS TO PRAY TO GOD, THE HOLY ONE
AND CAUSE THEIR BROTHERS AND SISTERS IN CHRIST, TO REST IN THE SPIRIT
AND SING TO THE LORD A NEW SONG, AND LET THE WHOLE WORLD HEAR IT
THEY SHALL WALK IN THE LIGHT OF CHRIST, AND SHALL EXALT HIS NAME
GOD, HIMSELF, TOOK ON OUR FLESH AND FOR OUR SINS, BORE THE BLAME
THEY SHALL ALWAYS STRIVE TO BE HOLY AND LOVE ONE ANOTHER
FOR CHRIST, WHO DIED FOR US, IS OUR LORD, AND OUR BROTHER
AND SO I SAY TO YOU, MY BROTHERS, MY SISTERS, MY DEAR FRIENDS
IN NOMINE PATRIS, ET FILII, ET SPIRITUS SANTI, AMEN

TO THEE I SING, ALMIGHTY GOD

OH ALMIGHTY ETERNAL FATHER, TO THEE DO I SING
LET MY HANDS RAISE TO YOUR HEAVENS, LET THE MUSIC RING
TO YOU, MY KING, MY GOD, MIGHTY ONE WHO DWELLS ABOVE
ALMIGHTY POWER, ALMIGHTY MERCY, AND ALMIGHTY LOVE
TO YOU, MY HEAVENLY FATHER, I SING SONGS OF PRAISE
BECAUSE FROM LOWLY DEPTHS, YOUR DAUGHTER, YOU HAVE RAISED

THROUGH YOUR TENDER MERCY, OH GOD, MOST HOLY ONE,
WHEN I WAS BROKEN, WEAK AND WORN, YOU SENT YOUR ONLY SON
AND HE, THOUGH PURE AND SINLESS, MEEKLY BORE THE SHAME
BECAUSE I WAS LOST, HE PAID THE COST, OH PRAISE HIS HOLY NAME
TO YOU, OH HOLY SPIRIT, SENT TO GUIDE ME TO THE LIGHT,
HOLY, HOLY, HOLY LORD, GOD OF HEAVENLY DELIGHTS

TO THEE I SING ALMIGHTY GOD, FOR YOU HAVE FASHIONED ME
IN YOUR IMAGE AND YOUR LIKENESS, OH GOD WHO SETS ME FREE
THERE IS NO OTHER ABOVE YOU, THERE IS NO GREATER LOVE
EARTH, LORD, IS YOUR FOOTSTOOL, YOUR THRONE, THE HEAVENS ABOVE
WHEN MY FEEBLE EXISTANCE ENDS, WHEN MY TIME ON EARTH IS O'RE
MAY I STILL PRAISE WITH HANDS UPRAISED, MY GOD FOREVER MORE

WHERE ARE YOU, LORD

WHERE ARE YOU MY LORD, I FEEL PERSECUTED
LORD I AM SO FILLED WITH PAIN
MY LOVED ONES HAVE TURNED AGAINST ME
I TURN TO YOU, LORD, ONCE AGAIN
MY HEART IS HEAVY WITH THIS BURDEN
LIKE A SWORD THRUST THROUGH MY HEART
HATEFUL WORDS, THAT NOW PURSUE ME
FROM MY MIND, THEY WON'T DEPART

FORGIVE, ME LORD FOR FAILING TO DO
WHAT YOU TAUGHT, WHEN THEY STRUCK ME DOWN
I SHOULD HAVE TURNED THE OTHER CHEEK
AND NOT STRIKE BACK, AS I WAS BOUND
LORD TAKE AWAY MY HURT AND ANGER
GIVE ME PEACE, FORGIVENESS AND GRACE
I LAY IT NOW, AT THE FOOT OF YOUR CROSS
I CALL YOU LORD, OH COME WITH HASTE

LORD WHERE ARE YOU NOW, IN MY ANGUISH
I NEED YOUR GUIDANCE AND YOUR LOVE
TO HELP ME BANISH ALL THIS PAIN, LORD
SEND YOUR SPIRIT FROM ABOVE
I HAVE ONLY YOU LORD, TO DRY MY TEARS
ONLY YOU TO BANISH HURT PRIDE
LORD, I FEEL THE COMFORT OF YOUR PRESCENCE NOW
YOU ARE EVER STANDING BY MY SIDE

LORD, IN YOUR LOVE AND YOUR COMPASSION
YOU ARE ALWAYS THERE FOR ME
LORD YOU KNOW AND YOU ARE THE TRUTH
AND YOUR TRUTH SHALL SET ME FREE
YOU ARE WHERE YOU HAVE ALWAYS BEEN, LORD
WHERE YOU'LL BE TILL THE END OF TIME
YOU SHALL ALWAYS BE MY SAVIOR
PRECIOUS JESUS, LOVE DIVINE

SLAUGHTER OF THE INNOCENT

MY BELOVED CHILDREN, I WOULD SPEAK TO YOU, NOW
OF A DEED THAT IS AN ABOMINATION TO THE LORD
AND I WISH TO ACKNOWLEDGE MY FAITHFUL CHILDREN
WHO WORK DILIGENTLY AND ARE OF ONE ACCORD
YOUR CONSTANT PRAYERS AND YOUR SILENT WATCH
IN THIS MATTER, MY CHILDREN, HAS ACCOMPLISHED MUCH
IF EVEN ONE MOTHER, CHANGES HER MIND
YOU KNOW, HER HEART, YOU HAVE TOUCHED
IN YOUR PATIENT, NON-VIOLENT AND PRAYERFUL WAY
YOU TRY TO DO WHAT IS GOOD AND RIGHT
TO HELP THESE MOTHERS UNDERSTAND
THEY NEED THE WAY, THE TRUTH AND THE LIFE

IT PAINS YOU, AS IT PAINS YOUR LORD,
TO SEE THE INNOCENT SLAUGHTERED
WHO ARE THEY, WHO CARRY OUT THESE DEEDS
WHO TEAR AWAY MY SONS AND MY DAUGHTERS
ARE THEY GOD, THAT THEY CAN DECIDE WHO LIVES AND WHO DIES
WOE TO THOSE WHO SEEK TO DESTROY PRECIOUS LIFE
FOR THEY SHALL NOT COME INTO MY KINGDOM,
AND THEY SHALL HAVE SORROW, AND STRIFE
SOMEDAY THEY WILL HAVE TO BEAR THE BLAME
FOR THE BABIES THEY HAVE TORN FROM THE WOMB
FOR ONLY, I, HAVE CONTROL OVER LIFE AND DEATH
THE GUILTY, THEIR SOULS, THEY HAVE DOOMED

FOR EACH LITTLE BABE WHO IS BORN OF MAN
IS SENT BY YOUR GOD; AND IS PART OF HIS PLAN
WHO ARE THEY, WHO DECIDE THIS CHILD CAN NOT BE
FOR UPON CONCEPTION, INTO MY LITTLE ONES, MY SPIRIT, I BREATHE
THIS IS THE SLAUGHTER OF THE INNOCENT, THE LITTLE UNBORN
IT SHALL NOT GO UNPUNISHED, ON MY NAME, I HAVE SWORN
THERE ARE THOSE WHO WOULD GLADLY GIVE THEIR LOVE
TO THESE BEAUTIFUL SOULS, SENT FROM GOD ABOVE
RAISE THEM AS CHILDREN OF GOD, SO MY WILL SHALL BE DONE
WHO DECIDES WHO LIVES OR DIES, I AM THE ONLY ONE
I AM THE LORD, WHO GIVES LIFE, IT IS NOT MAN'S TO TAKE
SOON THEY SHALL LEARN, IT IS NOT THEIR DECISION TO MAKE

THE PATH TO HOLY WISDOM

GOD'S GREAT GIFT OF WISDOM, IS A MOST HOLY GIFT
FOR IT HELPS US TO STAY ON THE RIGHT PATH
AND WITH HIS HOLY WISDOM, OUR SOULS WILL LIFT
TO HIGHEST HEAVEN; WE SHALL BE SPARED GOD'S WRATH
PRAY ALWAYS TO OUR LORD, FOR FAITH AND HOPE,
FOR TRUST IN HIS PRECIOUS, BENEVOLENT AND ETERNAL LOVE
FOR THE SOUL WHO RELYS ON THESE GIFTS FROM GOD
RECEIVES DIVINE GRACE, FROM THE FATHER ABOVE
THERE IS THE GIFT OF FORGIVENESS, FOR CHRIST PAID THE COST
FOR THOSE SOULS WHO HAVE TRUE SORROW FOR SIN
JESUS OPENED HIS ARMS FOR US; GAVE HIS LIFE UPON THE CROSS
HE IS THE GATE FOR REPENTANT SINNERS TO ENTER IN

PRAY, MY BROTHERS AND SISTERS, FOR ALL THE GIFTS HE HAS FOR US
FOR FORGIVENESS, FOR COMPASSION, FOR HIS ABUNDANT GRACE,
HIS UNDYING LOVE FOR HIS CHILDREN, ASK WITH FAITH AND TRUST
FOR HE WANTS TO GIVE US ALL THAT WE NEED, TO BEHOLD HIS HOLY FACE
FEAR NOT, THE LORD IS WITH US, HIS HOLY SPIRIT DWELLS WITHIN
HE LONGS TO GIVE, AND LONGS TO SAVE HIS BELOVED FROM ALL SIN
HE IS WAITING FOR US TO ASK, WITH TRUSTING, CHILDLIKE HEARTS
KING OF KINGS, WHO DIED FOR US, OH LORD HOW GREAT THOU ART
WHEN OUR TIME ON EARTH IS DONE, WE SHALL GO WITHOUT FEAR
BECAUSE OUR LORD SHALL WELCOME US, FOR HE IS EVER NEAR
JESUS CHRIST, REDEEMER, LAMB OF GOD, SAVIOR WHOM WE ADORE
LEAD US ON THE PATH TO HOLY WISDOM, TO LOVE FOREVERMORE

JESUS, OUR SAVING LORD

JESUS CHRIST, ONLY BEGOTTEN SON OF THE LIVING GOD
WE GIVE YOU ALL GLORY, ALL HONOR AND PRAISE
FOR YOU ARE THE KING OF KINGS, AND LORD OF LORDS
NAME ABOVE ALL NAMES, AND OUR HIDING PLACE
YOU ARE ALL WE NEED, MOST HOLY FOUNTAIN OF JOY
YOU ARE OUR GREAT FORTRESS AND OUR STRONG SHIELD
THE FONT OF ALL HOLINESS, PRECIOUS LAMB WITHOUT BLEMISH
TO YOU AND ONLY YOU, MAY OUR SPIRITS YIELD

JESUS, PRECIOUS LAMB OF GOD, OUR STRENGTH AND OUR SONG
WE SHALL SING YOUR PRAISES ALL DAY AND ALL NIGHT LONG
PRINCE OF PEACE, BRIGHT MORNING STAR, LORD IN WHOM WE TRUST
WOUNDERFUL COUNCELOR, LOVE MOST PURE, EMMANUEL GOD WITH US
OUR JUSTIFICATION, OUR SALVATION, PROTECTOR OF THE WEAK
YOU SHALL ALWAYS BE THE ONE THAT WE, YOUR CHILDREN, SEEK
YOU ARE THE GOOD SHEPHERD, YOU ARE OUR COVENANT
OH GLORIOUS LIGHT OF THE WORLD, BY THE FATHER SENT

KING OF ALL CREATION, WE ARE SAVED BY YOUR MIGHTY POWER
FOR YOU ARE THE MIGHTY SON OF GOD, AND OUR STRONG TOWER
LORD OF HOSTS, ROCK OF AGES, UNIVERSAL BLESSED KING
YOU ARE THE WAY FOR ALL OUR LIFE, YOU ARE OUR EVERYTHING
OH MIGHTY AND HOLY WARRIOR, OUR REDEEMER, AND TRUE VINE
OUR SAVING GRACE, FONT OF WISDOM, UNENDING LOVE DIVINE
PRAISE BE ON OUR LIPS AND IN OUR HEARTS FOR OUR SAVING LORD
FOR YOU ARE OUR SURE SONG OF HOPE, OUR GOD WHOM WE ADORE

GIVE PRAISE UNTO THE LORD

GIVE PRAISE UNTO THE LORD, FOR HE IS GOOD
FOR HIS SPLENDOR AND MAJESTY HAVE NO END
HIS MERCY AND HIS KINDNESS HE FREELY GIVES
HE GAVE HIMSELF TO DEATH, SO THAT WE MIGHT LIVE
HIS HEART IS BURNING WITH LOVE FOR US
HE ASKS FOR OUR LOVE, HE ASKS FOR OUR TRUST
HE SHALL ALWAYS AND EVER GIVE US WHAT WE NEED
FOR THOSE FREED BY THE SON, ARE FREE INDEED
WE, AS HIS CHILDREN, MUST FOLLOW HIS GUIDING LIGHT
TO RESIST ALL SIN, TO FIGHT THE FIGHT
WE NEED OUR TRUE GOD'S AID, TO REACH OUR HEAVENLY HOME
WHERE WE MAY WORSHIP HIM AROUND THE GREAT THRONE

SO PRAISE HIS HOLY NAME, WORSHIP HIM EXCEEDINGLY
FOR IN HIM AND IN ONLY HIM, CAN WE BE SET FREE
CONFESS HIM, AS YOUR SAVIOR, SO TO WALK IN HIS LIGHT
HE SAVES HIS WAYWARD CHILDREN WITH HIS STRENGTH AND HIS MIGHT
HE IS OUR PRECIOUS SAVIOR, WHO CONQUERED DEATH AND SIN
HE BECAME THE GATE FOR HIS REDEEMED TO ENTER IN
HEAVENLY FATHER, WHO GAVE HIS ONLY BEGOTTEN SON
MAY WE PRAISE HIM FOREVER; RAISE OUR VOICES AS ONE
LET US CONCECRATE OURSELVES TO HIM EACH AND EVERY DAY
MAKE HIM KING OVER OUR LIVES, FOR HE IS THE ONLY WAY
AND HE IS TRUTH AND THE LIGHT, WHEREBY WE MAY ASCEND
TO DWELL WITH THE ONE TRUE LIVING GOD, ALLELUIA, AMEN

CHRIST OUR KING

OH LORD, AS I CONTEMPLATE ALL YOU HAVE DONE FOR US
MY HEART NEARLY BURSTS WITH JOY
FOR LONG AGO, WHEN THE TIME WAS FULFILLED
MARY BROUGHT FORTH HER BABY BOY
HE WAS A VERY SPECIAL CHILD, ONE BORN TO BE A KING
IN MY MIND AND IN MY HEART, I HEAR THE ANGELS SING
THEY SANG TO THE SHEPHERDS ON THE HILLS THAT WINTER DAY
"HOSANNA IN THE HIGHEST, PEACE ON EARTH, FEAR NOT", THEY SAY

"FOR UNTO YOU A KING IS BORN, OF A VIRGIN MEEK AND MILD
IN A MANGER, 'NEATH YON STAR, YOU SHALL FIND THE HOLY CHILD"
THE SHEPHERDS SAID, "LET US MAKE HASTE, TO SEE THE HOLY ONE
PROCLAIMED BY GOD'S PROPHETS; IT IS HIS ONLY BEGOTTEN SON"
AND SO THEY WENT TO BETHLEHEM, WITH JOY AND AWE THAT DAY
TO WORSHIP THE PROMISED ONE OF GOD, WHO IN A MANGER LAY
OH HOLY AND IMMORTAL GOD WE GIVE YOU THANKS AND PRAISE
BECAUSE YOU SENT YOUR HOLY SON, WHO WOULD LIGHT OUR WAY

CHRIST, OUR KING, OUR LORD AND GOD, BORN FOR ALL MANKIND
CAME AS OUR REDEEMER FOR THE LOST, THE SICK, THE BLIND
MARY, WHO WAS BLESSED OF GOD, A VIRGIN FLOWER LOWLY
AGREED TO BE THE MOTHER OF GOD, A CHILD PERFECT AND HOLY
JOSEPH, HER MOST CHASTE SPOUSE, PROTECTOR OF THEM BOTH
WOULD RAISE THE CHILD, AS HIS OWN SON, FOR THIS HE TOOK AN OATH
FINDING HIS BETROTHED, WAS WITH CHILD, TROUBLE TURNED TO AWE
FOR AN ANGEL SAID TO HIM; "FEAR NOT, SHE BEARS THE SON OF GOD"

THEN CAME THE HOLY NIGHT, WHEN THEY TRAVELLED TO BETHLEHEM
MARY WAS HEAVY WITH CHILD, BUT THERE WAS NO ROOM FOR THEM
AN INN KEEPER TOOK PITY, SEEING THE YOUNG GIRL SO WORN
HE SAID, "THERE IS THE STABLE, WHERE, AT LEAST, YOU SHALL BE WARM"
JOSEPH AND MARY THANKED HIM FOR HIS GENEROUSITY
A PLACE TO LAY THEIR HEADS, THANK YOU FATHER FOR THY MERCY
WHILE THEY WERE THERE, IN THE STABLE, THE BLESSED BABY CAME
AT LAST WAS BORN, CHRIST OUR KING, AND 'JESUS' IS HIS NAME

HOLY IS YOUR NAME

LORD, LET US ALWAYS SEEK TO WALK IN YOUR WAYS
AND LET US UNCEASINGLY PRAISE YOUR HOLY NAME
WE DESIRE ONLY, TO LIVE IN THE LIGHT OF YOUR LOVE
SING PRAISE FOR YOUR GOODNESS; FOR US, YOU BORE THE BLAME
WE WERE STAINED BY SIN; BY YOUR PRECIOUS BLOOD REDEEMED
AMAZING LOVE, YOU GAVE YOUR LIFE, OH HOLY IMMORTAL KING
WE WERE LOST, BUT NOW WE ARE FOUND BY YOUR AMAZING GRACE
YOU DIED, AND ROSE TO GLORY, SO WE MAY SEE YOUR HOLY FACE

MAY WE ALWAYS AND EVERYWHERE REJOICE IN YOU, OUR LORD
YOU SET THE CAPTIVES FREE; OH JESUS, WE THEE, ADORE
THOUGH INNOCENT HOLY LAMB OF GOD, YOU CAME TO SET US FREE
YOU ARE ALMIGHTY GOD WHO WAS AND IS, AND ALWAYS SHALL BE
AS IN THAT GREAT, HOLY SONG, WE WERE BLIND BUT NOW WE SEE
WERE LOST BUT NOW WE ARE FOUND, WITH YOU MAY WE EVER BE
WITH HEARTFELT LOVE, OH LORD, YOUR PRAISES WE DO SING
OH HOLY ANOINTED LAMB OF GOD, OUR LORD, OUR GOD AND KING

TO YOU, OH LORD, WE FOREVER SING WITH OUR HANDS UPRAISED
MAY ALL CREATION JOIN US, IN OUR MIGHTY SONGS OF PRAISE
FOR YOU ARE GOD, AND YOU ALONE, ARE OUR STRENGTH AND SONG
MAY ALL IN HEAVEN, ALL ON EARTH, BE MOVED TO SING ALONG
PRAISED BE OUR GOD, ON THE HILLS, IN THE VALLEYS AND THE SEAS
TO OUR SAVING LORD, WHO WAS, AND IS, AND WILL EVER BE
FOR YOU SO LOVED THE WORLD, YOU CAME AND BORE OUR SHAME
WE THANK YOU, PRECIOUS LAMB OF GOD, HOLY IS YOUR NAME

HATE NOT THE SINNER, BUT THE SIN

MY DEAREST SAVIOR, MY LORD, AND MY GOD WHO SAVES
I THANK YOU SO MUCH, FOR WHAT YOU HAVE REVEALED TO ME
IN YOUR ABUNDANT LOVE, YOUR AMAZING GRACE, YOUR HOLY WAYS
YOU HAVE REVEALED TO ME HOW I MAY BE FOREVER SET FREE
FOR SO LONG NOW, I HAVE PRAYED FOR AND BEEN PRAYED UPON
FOR HEALING AND FOR WHOLENESS FROM SICKNESS AND FROM PAIN
BUT THERE WERE SO MANY THINGS FROM CHILDHOOD AND BEYOND
TRAPPED BY BETRAYAL, THAT HURT ME AGAIN AND AGAIN
THIS REVELATION, LORD, HAS CAUSED ME TO WELCOME TOMORROW
FOR LORD, WITH YOUR WORDS, YOU HAVE CAST OFF MY SORROW
GOOD JESUS YOU HAVE TAUGHT ME HOW TO GAIN PEACE WITHIN
YOU SAID TO ME "MY CHILD, HATE NOT THE SINNER, BUT THE SIN"

I CANNOT EXPRESS, THE INCREDIBLE PEACE THIS REVELATION GIVES
FOR TOO MANY YEARS, THESE HURTS HAVE REIGNED OVER MY LIFE
MOST HOLY SAVIOR, WHO DIED AND ROSE AND FOREVER LIVES
YOU HAVE SET ME FREE, TAKEN MY BURDENS, DISPELLED THE STRIFE
NOW I CAN TRULY LAY MY PAST HURTS, MY SICKNESS AND MY PAIN
AT THE FOOT OF YOUR HOLY CROSS, NEVER, NEVER TO RETURN
YOU SPOKE TO MY SOUL, WORDS THAT HAVE BECOME A REFRAIN
SO THAT, NOT HURT, BUT LOVE FOR MY GOD, IN MY HEART BURNS
YOU HAVE GIVEN ME POWER TO CAST OFF THE THINGS FROM THE PAST
WONDERFUL, POWERFUL, LIVING GOD, YOUR SPIRIT DWELLS WITHIN
YOU HAVE GIVEN ME A GIFT OF PEACE, THAT WILL FOREVER LAST
BY INSTRUCTING ME TO HATE, NOT THE SINNER, BUT THE SIN

THANK YOU, HEAVENLY FATHER

OH DEAR HEAVENLY FATHER, I THANK YOU EXCEEDINGLY
FOR ALL YOU, MY GOD ALMIGHTY, HAVE DONE FOR ME
YOU HAVE GRACIOUSLY TAUGHT ME HOW TO LIVE MY LIFE
YOU HAVE BROUGHT ME THROUGH GREAT TRIALS AND GREAT STRIFE
YOU SENT YOUR PRECIOUS SON, THE LIVING WORD, MADE FLESH
THE WAY, THE TRUTH AND THE LIFE, WHO CAME TO GIVE ME REST
THERE IS NO WAY I CAN COMPARE, ANYTHING IN THIS WORLD
TO MY PRECIOUS SAVIOR, WHO CAME WITH SACRED ARMS UNFURLED
I CAN ONLY KNEEL, IN HUMBLE PRAYER, TO THANK MY HEAVENLY KING
AND TELL YOU, LORD, THAT YOU ARE MY ALL, MY ROCK, MY EVERYTHING

THANK YOU, JESUS, FOR LOVING ME, SO THAT NOW I MAY LIVE
FOR YOU HELPED ME TO HATE THE SINS, AND SINNERS TO FORGIVE
FOR IF I CANNOT FORGIVE THOSE WHO HAVE OFFENDED ME
HOW CAN I ASK FORGIVENESS FOR THE TIMES I'VE OFFENDED THEE
CREATE IN ME, I BEG OF YOU, LORD, A NEW, CLEAN, PURE HEART
SO THAT FROM YOU, THE LIVING GOD, MY SOUL SHALL NOT DEPART
MAY I ALWAYS AND EVERYWHERE SING PRAISES TO YOU, MY GOD
FATHER, SON AND HOLY SPIRIT, WHO FILLS MY SOUL WITH AWE
FOR WHO IS THERE LIKE YOU, MY LORD, IN WHOM I TRUST
THERE IS NO OTHER ABOVE YOU, LORD, WHO MADE ME FROM THE DUST

TODAY, I HUMBLY DEDICATE ALL THAT I AM, ALL I HAVE, TO THEE
GLADLY I WOULD USE THE GIFTS THAT YOU HAVE GIVEN ME
TO SERVE YOU, MY PRECIOUS SAVING GOD, WITH ALL OF MY MIGHT
YOU GAVE YOUR ONLY BEGOTTEN SON, WITH WHOM THERE IS NO NIGHT
YOU HAVE SHOWN ME HOW, MY LORD, TO WALK AWAY AT LAST
FOR INTO THE SEA OF FORGETFULNESS, MY HURTS I CAN NOW CAST
FOR LORD, I KNOW, JUST AS I KNOW, THAT YOU FOREVER LIVE
FROM PAST HURTS, I AM FOREVER FREE, FOR I CAN SAY, "I FORGIVE"
MY GOD, MAY I CONSTANTLY THIRST FOR YOUR MOST HOLY PRESENCE
UNTIL AT LAST I BEHOLD YOU IN YOUR MAJESTIC MAGNIFICENCE

WHOM SHALL I FEAR

WITH GOD BY MY SIDE, WHOM SHALL I FEAR
FOR I SHALL TURN TO HIM, WHO IS EVER NEAR
FROM THE MALIGNANT ENEMY, MY HOLY GOD SHALL SAVE
ALL WHO LOVE AND FEAR HIM, WHO BECAME A SLAVE
FOR WITH A MIGHTY SWORD, THE HOLY ONE SHALL REAP
AND CAST INTO THE FIERY PIT, UNREPENTANT SHEEP
WITH A MIGHTY SHOUT, AND A MIGHTY TRUMPET BLAST
THE HOLY ONE, OUR REDEEMING LORD, SHALL RETURN AT LAST
IN THE SAME MANNER AS HE WAS SEEN ASCENDING INTO HEAVEN
SO SHALL HE RETURN, AT THE APPOINTED TIME GIVEN
ONLY THE HEAVENLY FATHER KNOWS, FOR IT HIS BY HIS WILL
THAT THE ANOINTED ONE SHALL RETURN, PROPHECY TO FULFILL

SO WE MUST KEEP WATCH, TO STAY IN HIS HOLY GRACE
BECAUSE WE DO NOT KNOW THE TIME NOR THE PLACE
WHEN OUR MIGHTY SAVIOR, TO THIS WORLD SHALL RETURN
TO SORT THE WHEAT FROM THE CHAFF WHICH SHALL BE BURNED
HIS BELOVED SHALL WITNESS, THE PRECIOUS LAMB UPON THE THRONE
WHO CAME INTO THE WORLD, TO MAKE MANKIND HIS OWN
FOR HE WHO HOLDS CREATION, IN HIS MIGHTY HAND
PAID THE COST TO SAVE THE LOST, IN KEEPING WITH THE DIVINE PLAN
OH LIVING, LOVING GOD, YOU SAVE YOUR CHILDREN FROM THEIR SINS
TO RESCUE US FROM THE DARK NIGHT, SO THAT WE MAY ENTER IN
THE GATEWAY, WHO IS THE LORD, WHO EVER REMAINS NEAR
WITH YOU, MY LORD, BY MY SIDE, WHOM THEN, SHALL I FEAR

THE ABSENCE OF LIGHT

LORD OF ALL, MOST HOLY LIGHT OF THE WORLD
YOU WHO CAME TO SET THE CAPTIVES FREE
HOW LOST WOULD BE YOUR CHILDREN,
IF YOU WERE NOT OUR GOD, ETERNALLY
FOR WE ARE NOTHING WITHOUT YOU, LORD
WE WOULD BE IN SUCH TERRIBLE PLIGHT
OH MY LORD, I PRAY, NEVER ABANDON US
FOR YOUR ABSENCE LORD, WOULD BE THE ABSENCE OF LIGHT

EVIL WOULD OVERTAKE YOUR LOVED ONES
WITHOUT YOUR PROTECTION, TO KEEP US PURE
THOUGH THERE IS EVIL IN THIS WORLD
SO THERE IS GOOD, THE ONES WHO, THEE, ADORE
LORD, NEVER FORSAKE US, YOUR CHILDREN
FOR WE WOULD BE BLINDED, WE'D HAVE NO SIGHT
WITHOUT YOUR HOLY PRESENCE, LORD, WE WOULD BE LOST
FOR YOUR ABSENCE LORD, WOULD BE THE ABSENCE OF LIGHT

PRAISE, OH PRAISE, YOUR HOLY NAME, ROYAL KING OF LOVE AND LIGHT
RETURNING FROM WHENCE YOU CAME, TO TAKE YOUR RIGHTFUL PLACE
LEAVING YOUR PROMISE TO THE FAITHFUL, WHOM YOU DEARLY LOVE
TO SEND YOUR SPIRIT AMONG US, TO GUIDE US, IN HOLY GRACE
AND YOU PROMISED TO BE WITH US, FOR ALL ETERNITY
HAPPY ARE YOUR CHILDREN, BORN AGAIN IN YOUR HOLY SIGHT
FILLED WITH YOUR HOLY SPIRIT, ABUNDANTLY BLESSED ARE WE
FOR YOUR ABSENCE LORD, WOULD BE THE ABSENCE OF LIGHT

TEACH US LORD

TEACH US LORD, IN ALL YOUR WAYS, GIVE US KNOWLEDGE
AND UNDERSTANDING, INCREASE OUR FAITH, INCREASE OUR LOVE
FOR WE WANT TO GO DEEPER AND DEEPER WITH YOU
POUR DOWN YOUR BLESSINGS FROM ABOVE
WE YEARN TO WALK IN YOUR MOST HOLY WAYS
ONLY IN YOU, LORD, DO WE PLACE OUR TRUST
LET US WALK ALWAYS IN YOUR HOLY LIGHT
LORD OF LORDS, KING OF KINGS, SO GRACIOUS TO US

SUFFER US NOT TO BE SEPARATED FROM YOU, OUR SAVING LORD,
GRACIOUSLY HIDE US IN YOUR HOLY WOUNDS, FOR SATAN IS EVER NEAR
WAITING TO STEAL OUR IMMORTAL SOULS FROM HE WHOM WE ADORE
BUT IN YOU WE SHALL BE SAFE, OH GOD, WE SHALL NOT CRINGE IN FEAR
OUR SOLACE IS IN YOUR HOLY WORD, SPOKEN FROM THY HOLY LIPS
WORDS OF WISDOM, WORDS OF LOVE, SHOWING THE WAY TO WORSHIP
EVER WATCHING OVER YOUR CHILDREN, READY TO TAKE OUR HANDS
TO LEAD US IN THE PATH OF RIGHTEOUSNESS, OH HOLY PRECIOUS LAMB

BRING US EVER DEEPER IN THE INDWELLING OF YOUR HOLY SPIRIT
FOR WE LONG TO SPREAD YOUR HOLY WORD, FOOD FOR LIFE
AND TO PRAISE YOUR HOLY NAME, SAVING GOD, BORN AS MAN
PRAISE YOU HOLY, LIVING GOD, WHO SAVES US FROM ALL STRIFE
TEACH US OH GOD ETERNAL, SO LOVING AND SO KIND
WHO SENT HIS SON, THE CHOSEN ONE, WHO CAME TO RANSOM US
THROUGH YOUR CHIILDREN, YOU HEAL THE SICK THE LAME THE BLIND
THUS, SHOWING YOUR MIGHTY POWER, HOLY GOD IN WHOM WE TRUST

IN YOUR HAND

LORD HOW FULL OF DARKNESS HAS BECOME THE WORLD YOU HAVE MADE
BUT YOUR EVERLASTING LIGHT SHINES THROUGH TO THOSE WHO SEEK
YOU DID NOT MAKE THIS WORLD FOR DARKNESS, YOU MADE IT FOR JOY
MAN, IN WHOM YOU PLACED ITS CARE, WERE, BY SIN, MADE WEAK
LORD, WE YOUR CHILDREN, MUST PAY HEED TO THE DESIRE YOU PLACE
INSIDE OUR HEARTS, THAT SPURS US ON TO CONSTANTLY SEEK YOUR FACE
THE IMPULSE TO PURSUE YOU, OUR LORD AND OUR GOD
COMES FROM YOU, ALMIGHTY LORD OF HEAVEN AND OF EARTH
WE ARE MADE BY YOU, TO WORSHIP YOU, UNTIL THE END OF TIME
SO WE SEEK TO FIND YOU LORD, LO---, EVEN FROM OUR BIRTH
WE FOREVER THIRST FOR YOU, LORD, BUT WE MUST UNDERSTAND
THAT WHILE WE ARE PURSUING YOU, WE ARE ALREADY IN YOUR HAND

WE ARE MADE IN YOUR IMAGE, LORD, YOU PLACED WITHIN OUR SOULS
THE CAPACITY TO KNOW YOU, OH GOD, BUT IN SIN, WE LACK THE POWER
TO RECOGNIZE OUR KINSHIP WITH THE LORD WHO MAKES US WHOLE
WE FAIL TO KNOW, AS WE SHOULD, OUR GOD, OUR ONE STRONG TOWER
FORGIVING LORD, YOU LOVINGLY GRANT OUR SOULS REGENERATION
THEN OUR BEING SENSES OUR KINSHIP, AND LEAPS WITH RECOGNITION
FOR LORD, YOU MADE US TO WORSHIP YOU, IN OBEDIENCE AND IN TRUST
AND TO PRAISE THE HOLIEST OF NAMES, THEN YOU, IN TURN, BLESS US
WE MUST ALWAYS SEEK YOU LORD, BUT WE MUST UNDERSTAND
THAT WHILE WE ARE PURSUING YOU, WE ARE ALREADY IN YOUR HAND

JESUS, HOLY LIVING BREAD

OH JESUS, HOLY LIVING BREAD, HOW SWEET THY TASTE
FROM THY HOLY FOUNTAINHEAD, WE QUENCH OUR THIRST
WE DARE TO APPROACH THE LIVING GOD. WITH HASTE
F0R YOU, OUR GOD AND SAVIOR, HAVE LOVED US FIRST
OH LORD, THY SACRED HEART DOTH BURN WITH LOVE
FOR THY WAYWARD CHILDREN, WHOM THOU HAST REDEEMED
YOU, OUR LIVING, HOLY GOD, DESCENDED FROM ABOVE
TO THWART THE WICKED ENEMY'S EVIL SCHEMES
YOU LEAD YOUR CHILDREN, GENTLY, ON THE PATH
SENT BY THE FATHER, YOU CAME TO SHOW THE WAY
LOVINGLY, MERCIFULLY, YOU SAVE US FROM THE WRATH
OH MERCIFUL SAVIOR, KEEP US SAFE, WE PRAY

OH MOST HIGH GOD, YOU ARE OUR TREASURED ONE
ONLY BEGOTTEN SON OF THE FATHER, LOVE DIVINE
SPIRIT OF JESUS, SANCTIFY OUR IMMORTAL SOULS
BODY OF CHRIST, WE PRAY 'FEED THOSE WHO ARE THINE'
BLOOD OF CHRIST, WHICH INEBRIATES
OVERCOMING OUR SPIRITS WITH JOYOUS SONG
OF THY SWEET GRACE, WHICH THOU DOST FREELY GIVE
WE PRAISE THEE LORD, AND SHALL, OUR WHOLE LIFE LONG
LORD MAY WE TASTE THY GOODNESS FOR ALL OF OUR LIVES
AND MAY WE ALWAYS AND EVER THIRST FOR THEE
FOR WE ARE LESS THAN NOTHING WITHOUT OUR LORD
THE LIVING WORD, WHO SETS HIS CHILDREN FREE

THANK YOU LORD, FOR FREEING ME

OH LORD, I THANK YOU FOR SHOWING ME THE WAY
TO LET THY BLESSED HEALING TOUCH MY HEART TODAY
DEEP, DARK, UNSPOKEN THINGS I COULD NOT NAME OR UNDERSTAND
WERE WITH ME ALWAYS UNTIL YOU EXTENDED YOUR BLESSED HANDS
SOMETIMES WE ONLY REALIZE LONG AFTER WE MATURE
MEMORIES OF CHILDHOOD THAT OUR MINDS COULD NOT ENDURE
LORD, YOU HAVE GIVEN ME LOVE FAR BEYOND MEASURE
YOU HAVE GIVEN ME NEW MEMORIES; ONES THAT I MAY TREASURE
YOU HAVE GRACIOUSLY OFFERED TO LET ME FREELY TOSS
MY HURTS, PAST TERRORS, AND PAIN, TO THE FOOT OF YOUR HOLY CROSS

YOU HAVE TAUGHT ME TO FORGIVE, AS YOU HAVE FORGIVEN ME
FROM ALL THE HURTS OF MY YOUNG PAST, YOU HAVE SET ME FREE
YOU SAID, "MY CHILD, FORGIVING THOSE WHOSE DEEDS BE DARK AS NIGHT
IS NOT TELLING THOSE THAT HURT YOU, THAT THEIR MISDEEDS WERE RIGHT
INSTEAD, LITTLE ONE, YOU ARE, INDEED, TAKING BACK YOUR POWER
SO MEMORIES, CAN NOT HAUNT YOU EVERY DAY OR EVERY HOUR
GIVE YOUR BURDENS UNTO ME, YOUR SAVIOR AND YOUR FRIEND
AND KNOW, MY CHILD, THAT I SHALL BE WITH YOU UNTIL THE END"

I THANK YOU LORD, FOR FREEING ME, FOREVER I SHALL PRAISE
AND SING WITH JOYFUL HEART, MY HANDS, TO HEAVEN, RAISED
YOU HAVE EASED MY BURDEN, RELEAVED ME OF GREAT STRESS
YOU HAVE SENT MY HURTFUL MEMORIES TO THE SEA OF FORGETFULNESS
I SING PRAISES TO THE HOLY NAME OF JESUS, MY SAVING LORD
WHO'S PROMISE TO ALL WHO LOVE HIM, IS GREAT AND BOUNDLESS REWARD
OH GOD, MY STRENGTH, MY SALVATION, AND ENDLESS JOY TO ME
I SAY WITH ALL MY HEART, THANK YOU, LORD, FOR FREEING ME

Elizabeth Ann Marks

IF YOU ONLY KNEW

MY CHILDREN, MY BELOVED ONES, IF YOU ONLY KNEW
WHAT WONDERFUL GLORIOUS THINGS, I HAVE IN STORE FOR YOU
HEAVEN'S DELIGHTS THAT SHALL BE MY LITTLE ONES' REWARD
YOU WOULD NEVER CEASE SINGING YOUR PRAISES TO THE LORD
FOR IN MY KINGDOM YOU SHALL FIND BEAUTY BEYOND COMPARE
IF YOU COULD ONLY FATHOM THE PEACE THAT AWAITS YOU THERE
LOVE BEYOND ALL UNDERSTANDING, FAR BEYOND MAN'S IMAGINATION
THERE ARE NO WORDS, THAT CAN DESCRIBE, THE REWARDS OF SALVATION

THE AWESOME BEAUTY, IN HEAVEN, MAN'S MIND COULD NEVER GRASP
UNTIL YOU ENTER HEAVEN'S DOOR, HOME WITH ME AT LAST
I GAVE YOU EARTH, FOR YOUR DOMAIN, MY CREATION, IT IS TRUE
BUT IT CAN NOT COMPARE TO THE WONDERS, THAT HEAVEN HOLDS FOR YOU
ALL BEAUTY UPON THE EARTH, CAN NOT CONTAIN OR MEASURE
WHAT YOU SHALL FIND IN PARADISE; YOU SHALL HAVE SUCH TREASURES
YOUR UNDERSTANDING CAN NOT IMAGINE THE RICHES YOU SHALL SEE
FOLLOW THE LORD IN ALL YOU DO, AND YOU SHALL DWELL WITH ME

YOU SHALL AT LAST BE MEETING, YOUR LORD OF SAVING GRACE
THEN, HE SHALL TAKE YOU HOME, WHERE YOU SHALL KNOW YOUR PLACE
THAT I, YOUR GOD, HAVE PREPARED FOR YOU IN MY HEAVENLY HOME
FOR MY MANSION HAS MANY ROOMS, ABOVE THE EARTH'S BLUE DOME
FEAR NOT, MY CHILDREN, DEVOTED ONES, FOR YOU SHALL COME TO ME
TO SHARE THE REWARDS I HAVE PREPARED FOR THOSE I HAVE SET FREE
WHEN YOU ARRIVE, YOU WILL KNOW THAT YOU HAVE AT LAST COME HOME
AND YOU SHALL JOYFULLY WORSHIP AT YOUR SAVIOR'S GREAT THRONE

(NOTE: THE FOLLOWING THREE POEMS, WERE PREVIOUSLY PUBLISHED WITH POETRY.COM AND ARE IN MEMORY OF MY MOTHER. THE FIRST ONE (AN ANGEL) IS PUBLISHED IN A BOOK CALLED "COLLECTED WHISPERS" THE SECOND, (MOTHER WENT HOME), IN A BOOK CALLED "THE COLORS OF LIFE), THE THIRD, "PRECIOUS MEMORIES OF MOTHER) IN A BOOK CALLED "THE SILENT JOURNEY". THERE ARE A FEW CHANGES, WHICH I MADE, TO MAKE THE MEANING MORE CLEAR TO THE READER. I SINCERELY HOPE THAT ALL WHO HAVE LOST A PARENT, OR ANY LOVED ONE, WHO LIVED THEIR LIVES IN THE LIGHT OF CHRIST, KNOW THAT THEY ARE SAFE, WITH HIM, OUR SAVING GOD)

DEDICATIONS

I WOULD LIKE TO DEDICATE THIS BOOK TO THE POWERFUL "CROWN OF GLORY" PRAYER GROUP. IT'S LEADER'S, KEVIN ROY, HIS MOM, THERESA ROY, HIS DAD, GEORGE ROY, HIS WIFE DEBBY ROY. I ALSO WOULD LIKE TO DEDICATE THIS TO BROTHER JACK, WHO HAS AMAZING FAITH, AND ALSO IN MEMORY OF HIS DEAR MOTHER, RITA, WHOM JACK HAS JUST RECENTLY LOST. I AM SURE SHE IS HAPPY RIGHT NOW WITH THE LORD. I WOULD LIKE TO INCLUDE IN THIS DEDICATION ALL THE POWERFUL PRAYER WARRIORS, THROUGH WHOM GOD WORKS TO BRING HEALING AND WHOLENESS TO HIS CHILDREN. I ALSO WOULD LIKE TO DEDICATE THIS BOOK TO MY BELOVED HUSBAND, 'REGINALD MARKS, MY CHILDREN, GEORGINA GRANT, ROSIE WHITE, KATHLEEN BENNETT, ANTHONY WHITE (jr.) AND FRANK WHITE, MY YOUNGEST. I WOULD ALSO LIKE TO DEDICATE THIS BOOK TO MY GRANDCHILDREN, SHANNON GRANT, THOMAS GRANT, JACQUELINE GRANT, BEN CYR, REGGIE BENNETT, JADE BENNETT, MICHAEL WHITE, ALEX WHITE, AND McKAILA DUPLISEA, ZACHARY WHITE, AND MY FIRST GREAT GRANDCHILD, AUDREY JANE CHATTERTON. LAST, BUT NOT LEAST, I DEDICATE THIS BOOK TO MY BEST FRIEND JACQUELINE LEWIS AND HER HUSBAND BILL LEWIS.

AN ANGEL

AN ANGEL CAME TO EARTH ONE DAY
GOD SENT HER DOWN, A WHILE TO STAY
TO LIVE HER LIFE WITH US, MERE MORTALS
AND BACK TO HEAVEN, EARN HER WAY
THROUGH TRIAL AND TRIBULATION,
SHE BRAVELY BORE HER CROSS
THE PIERCING SWORDS OF LIFE SHE BORE
WITH FAITH, SHE NEVER LOST
GOD SENT HER SEVERAL CHILDREN
TO GUIDE ALONG THE WAY
SHE DID HER BEST TO TEACH THEM WELL
IN HOW TO LIVE EACH DAY
SHE WAS LEFT WITHOUT HER SPOUSE
QUITE EARLY IN HER LIFE
BUT STILL SHE STROVE TO CARRY ON
THROUGH POVERTY AND STRIFE
BUT HER FAITH KEPT HER ON THE PATH
IN GOD, SHE'D TRUST, NO OTHER,
AND NOW SHE RESTS IN THE ARMS OF CHRIST
I'M PROUD TO CALL HER 'MOTHER'

MOTHER WENT HOME

MOTHER, AM I EVER AGAIN TO SEE YOUR FACE?
HAVE YOU LEFT ME BEHIND WITH NOT A TRACE
WE LAID YOU TO REST IN A DRESS OF BLUE
IT SEEMED THE ANGELS WERE CALLING YOU
THE SERVICE IS OVER, I NOW LAY ON MY BED
SUDDENLY A VISION COMES INTO MY HEAD
THOUGH, IN THIS VISION I BEHOLD TONIGHT
YOU ARE BEAUTIFULLY CLAD IN A ROBE OF WHITE
I KNOW THAT THIS IS NOT A MISTAKE
I KNOW THAT I AM FULLY AWAKE
I SEE YOU FLYING, AS IF WITH WINGS
I CAN'T BELIEVE, I AM SEENG THESE THINGS
ON A CLOUD YOU LAND, TO JESUS YOU RUN
THERE HE STANDS, AS BRIGHT AS THE SUN
WHEN YOU REACH HIM, YOU FALL DOWN ON YOUR KNEES
ON HIS HEAD, A CROWN OF DIAMONDS YOU SEE
IN THE CENTER OF THE CROWN, THERE IS A CROSS
FOR HE DIED, AND ROSE AGAIN, FOR OUR CAUSE,
IN A BRILLIANT WHITE ROBE WITH A SASH OF BLUE
HE SMILES GENTLY AND HE SPEAKS TO YOU
"ARISE, MY CHILD, AND COME WITH ME
TO MEET THE REST OF THE FAMILY
HOW HAPPY I FEEL NOW, AND FILLED WITH AWE
FOR WE KNOW, MOTHER, THAT YOU ARE SAFE WITH GOD

PRECIOUS MEMORIES OF MOTHER

CUDDLED UP ON MOTHER'S KNEE,
FEELING WARM AND SO SECURE,
IS IT REAL, THIS MEMORY?
YES, I AM ALMOST SURE
HOW I REMEMBER THE WARM EMBRACE
HER GENTLE TOUCH AS SHE KISSED MY FACE
AND FROM MY EYES, SHE HID HER PAIN
AS SHE SANG HER SAD REFRAIN
KNOWING THE TASK THAT WAS AHEAD
SINCE, MY DAD, HER HUSBAND, WAS DEAD
WITHOUT HIM, SHE WAS ALL ALONE
FOR EIGHT CHLDREN, SHE MUST MAKE A HOME
FOR I WAS JUST BABE, YOU SEE,
HER YOUNGEST CHILD, THE LAST TO BE
AND TO HIS MEMORY, SHE WOULD EVER BE TRUE
SHE STAYED SINGLE HER WHOLE LIFE THROUGH
THERE WAS STRUGGLE, HARDSHIPS AND MUCH STRIFE
BUT SHE MADE US, HER CHILDREN, HER LIFE
AND LIFE THREW HER CURVES, MOST EVERY DAY
BUT TRUST IN GOD, SHOWED HER THE WAY

Note: This poem is dedicated to my daughter, who was facing tremendous stress at the time. I tried to raise her spirits with this poem. I love you Roseann, and I am sorry things are not good between us at this time. I have placed my sorrow over this at the foot of the Holy Cross. I gave it to Jesus because I can't go on being depressed and crying all the time when I think of my beautiful daughters. I will keep all of you in my prayers, always..

MY GOLDEN GIRL

MY BABY GIRL SO TINY,
BLUE EYES SHINING SO BRIGHT
MY SWEET LITTLE BABY GIRL
WITH SKIN SO VERY WHITE
LIKE A WHITE ROSE YOU DID APPEAR
YOU WERE SO BEAUTIFUL AND SO FAIR
SO PERFECTLY FORMED, MY LITTLE ONE,
DELICATE, TINY FINGERS AND TINY TOES
WHAT OTHER NAME COULD FIT SO WELL,
I CALLED YOU MY LITTLE ROSE
AND SO I COMBINED YOUR NAME WITH MINE
I THOUGHT ROSEANN ELIZABETH WOULD BE FINE
YOU WERE BORN SO DELICATE,
OH PRECIOUS CHILD OF MINE
WITH FLAXEN HAIR AND EYES SO BLUE
AND LIPS LIKE CHERRY WINE
THOSE LOVELY EYES THAT SEE NOT WELL
A DEFECT AT YOUR BIRTH
KNOW, LITTLE ONE, IT DOES NOT DETRACT
ONE IOTA FROM YOUR WORTH
YOU RISE ABOVE IT ALL MY CHILD
YOU FILL MY HEART WITH PRIDE
YOU CONQUERED EVERY OBSTACLE
FROM CHALLENGE, DO NOT HIDE
THOUGH YOUR VISION WAS VERY POOR
IT DID NOT AFFECT YOUR SPIRIT
WHERE DID YOU FIND SUCH STRENGTH MY CHILD
FROM WHOM DID YOU INHEIRIT
YOUR INNER SPIRIT WAS BREATHED INTO YOU
BY OUR POWERFUL GOD, WHO REMAINS TRUE
FOR ALL YOU HAVE ACCOMPLISHED
WHATEVER WE'VE BEEN THROUGH
DEAREST ONE, YOU NEED TO KNOW
THAT I AM SO PROUD OF YOU
YOU FACED IMMENSE BETRAYAL
BETRAYAL OF THE WORST KIND
BUT YOU DUG DEEP, MY DEAREST ONE
MY GOLDEN GIRL STILL SHINES
KNOW, MY CHILD, THAT WHEREEVER YOU ARE
ONE THING IS SURELY TRUE
MY GOD WILL TAKE GOOD CARE OF YOU,
BECAUSE I ASKED HIM TO

SACRED HEART OF JESUS

MOST SACRED HEART OF JESUS, I CRY UNTO THEE
HAVE MERCY ON YOUR SERVANT AND FROM SICKNESS SET ME FREE
I WANT TO BE FREE TO SERVE YOU LORD, EACH AND EVERY DAY
BUT THIS ILLNESS, CRIPPLES MY ABILITIES, IN EACH AND EVERY WAY
I SEEK TO GO DEEPER INTO THE INDWELLING OF YOUR HOLY SPIRIT
WEAR MY FAITH LIKE A BURNING FLAME AND WITH OTHERS, SHARE IT
LORD, THIS CONDITION CAUSES ME SO MUCH STRESS AND STRIFE
IT OVERTAKES MY MIND, I CAN'T LIVE A NORMAL LIFE
NORMAL LIFE TO ME, MEANS PRACTICING MY FAITH
TO LIVE IN YOUR BLESSED HOLY LIGHT, SO TO REACH HEAVEN'S GATE
OH LORD, I BELIEVE THAT YOU CAN HEAL ME AT ANY TIME
FOR YOU ARE THE BLESSED PHYSICIAN, YOU ARE LOVE DIVINE

OH SACRED HEART OF JESUS, FROM WHOM ALL LOVE IS BORN
I VENERATE AND WORSHIP YOU, OH HOLY LOVE DIVINE
IF I COULD ONLY TOUCH THE HEM OF A ROBE YOU HAVE WORN
I BELIEVE, MY ROYAL KING, HEALING WOULD BE MINE
MANY ARE YOUR FAITHFUL SERVANTS, WHO PRAY AND PRAY FOR ME
THAT YOU MIGHT FROM ALL ILLNESS, CONSENT TO SET ME FREE
SO FILLED WITH YOUR HOLY LIGHT AND POWERFUL, MERCIFUL LOVE
I FEEL YOUR HOLY SPIRIT, AND PEACE SENT FROM ABOVE
O SACRED HEART, WITH EXPECTANT FAITH, I AWAIT THE WILL OF THEE
FOR I KNOW SURELY, AS YOU ARE MY GOD, THAT YOU WILL SET ME FREE
OH SACRED HEART OF JESUS, WHO SUFFERED FOR OUR SINS
MY HEART AND SOUL ARE OPEN, I PRAY THEE ENTER IN

THE DWELLING PLACE OF GOD

DO YOU HUNGER FOR THE PASSING THINGS OF THIS WORLD
THAT WHICH LEADS TO PAIN, MISERY AND DISCORD
DO YOU GO ABOUT SEARCHING FOR THAT WHICH YOU CAN NOT FIND
ARE YOUR EARS SO DEAF, ARE YOUR EYES SO BLIND
DO YOU KNOW WHAT YOU NEED TO EASE THE PAIN IN YOUR SOUL
TO EASE YOUR TROUBLED MIND, DO YOU NOT KNOW YOUR GOAL
YOU ARE HUNTING FOR PLEASURES IN THIS WICKED WORLD YOU TROD
ABANDON THOSE THINGS AND LOOK FOR THE DWELLINGPLACE OF GOD

DON'T YOU SEE THAT THE USELESS THINGS OF THIS WORLD
ARE JUST WISPS OF AIR SOON, LIKE SMOKE, AWAY THEY TWIRL
SEEK YE FIRST,   OUR PRECIOUS SAVIOR, WALK IN HIS HOLY LIGHT
WITH HIM IS FOUND JOY, A CALM SPIRIT, HE DISPELS THE DARK NIGHT
YOU WON'T HAVE TO TRAVEL FAR TO DISTANCE AND STRANGE LANDS
FOR WHILE YOU ARE SEARCHING FOR HIM, HE HOLDS YOU IN HIS HANDS
HE LOVES US SO MUCH, THAT FOR US HE CHOSE TO DIE
THOUGH ALMIGHTY AND ALL POWERFUL, HE CHOSE TO BE LIFTED HIGH

FOR PEACE, LOVE AND JOY FAR SURPASSING ANYTHING YOU CAN CONCEIVE
TASTE AND SEE THE GOODNESS OF THE LORD, WHO WAITS FOR THEE
HE IS ALWAYS AND EVER READY TO TAKE AWAY YOUR SINS
HE IS THE HOLY GATEWAY WHERE YOU MAY ENTER IN
NOW YOU MAY ASK," WHERE CAN I FIND THIS TREASURE TROVE OF LOVE
WHERE CAN I FIND THESE WONDROUS THINGS YOU SPEAK OF"
JUST INVITE HIM INTO YOUR LIFE, LET HIM BE THE ONE THAT YOU ADORE
HE SHALL ENTER INTO YOUR HEART AND YOU SHALL HUNGER NO MORE

SURELY, YOU WILL TASTE AND SEE THE GOODNESS OF THE LORD
WHERE THERE IS CONSOLATION, PEACE, JOY AND NO DISCORD
HE LOVES YOU WITH ALL HIS STRENGTH PROTECTS YOU FROM THE ENEMY
AND YOU SHALL SURELY BEND YOUR KNEE AND THANK HIM FITTINGLY
WHERE IN THIS WORLD OR BEYOND THE UNIVERSE IS THERE ONE LIKE HIM
WHO WOULD FOR OUR SAKES, CHOOSE TO DIE, TO RANSOM HIS CHILDREN
THE HOLY BLESSED TRINITY, WHO FILLS YOUR HEARTS WITH AWE
SHALL GIVE YOU A NEW, CLEAN, PURE HEART, THE DWELLINGPLACE OF GOD

BE NOT TROUBLED

BE NOT TROUBLED, MY LITTLE ONES, TRUST IN MY HOLY SPIRIT
YOU ARE FAVORED BY THE LORD, TAKE YOUR FAITH AND SHARE
FEAR NOT, THE EVIL ONE, MY CHILDREN, FOR YOU WALK IN MY LIGHT
YOU MUST TRUST YOUR LORD TO SAVE YOU FROM THE DARK NIGHT
KNOW THAT YOU ARE IN THIS WORLD, BUT YOU ARE NOT OF IT
YOU HAVE GIVEN YOURSLVES TO ME, MY GLORY, YOU SHALL INHEIRIT
CONTINUE TO WORK FOR THE GOOD OF SOULS, IN FAITH AND IN LOVE
YOU SHALL SURELY BE PRESENT WITH MY ANGELS AND SAINTS ABOVE
LOOK FOR SIGNS, WHICH SHALL PRECEDE THE COMING OF THE LORD
AND ALL SHALL BOW DOWN TO JESUS, TO WORSHIP AND ADORE

BE NOT TROUBLED, MY BELOVED, FOR YOU HAVE NOTHING TO FEAR
YOU ARE MY OWN DEAR CHILDREN; THE VOICE OF GOD, YOU HEAR
THE FAITHFUL ONES, WHOM I HAVE CHOSEN, FROM THIS SINFUL WORLD
SHALL NOT SUBMIT TO THE EVIL ONE, WHEN HIS FURY SHALL UNFURL
BUT KNOW, THAT I SHALL DEFEND YOU, MY CHILDREN OF THE LIGHT
YOU HAVE FOUGHT THE EVIL FOE, WHO COMES FROM DARKEST NIGHT
AND YOU SHALL SEE A NEW JERUSALEM, DESCENDING FROM THE HEAVENS
WHERE SHALL RULE THE MIGHTY KING, WHO FOR YOUR SINS WAS GIVEN
UNTO DEATH UPON A CROSS, TO SAVE THE WORLD FROM SIN
BUT HE WAS RAISED, AS WAS FORETOLD, TO USHER REDEMPTION IN
SO BE NOT TROUBLED, MY LITTLE ONES, MY BELOVED, DO NOT FEAR
FOR YOU ARE BLESSED ETERNALLY, FOR YOU, I SHALL BE NEAR

YOU WHO WALK IN MY HOLY LIGHT, SHALL GATHER ROUND MY THRONE
WHERE I SHALL EASE YOUR BURDENS; PARADISE SHALL BE YOUR HOME
NEVER A TEAR SHALL BE SHED, WITH ME THERE SHALL BE NO PAIN
NO HEARTACHES, NO LONELINESS, ONLY JOY AND GLAD REFRAIN
YOU SHALL JOIN THE HIGHEST CHOIRS, TO PRAISE MY HOLY NAME
YOU SHALL BEHOLD THE PRECIOUS LAMB, WHO, TO YOU, GLADLY CAME
TO FORFEIT HIS LIFE UPON THE CROSS, HIS PRECIOUS BLOOD TO SHED
TO SAVE HIS CHILDREN FROM THEIR SINS, BECAME THE LIVING BREAD
WOE TO THOSE WHO SCORN HIM, THE HOLY WORD MADE FLESH
THEY SHALL REAP WHAT THEY HAVE SOWN; AND THEY SHALL HAVE NO REST
CHILDREN, YOU MUST LET THEM KNOW THAT THEIR SAVIOR AWAITS
FOR THEM TO REPENT AND RETURN TO HIM, LEST IT BE TOO LATE

HEAVEN'S GATE

MY CHILDREN, I, YOUR LORD AND SAVIOR OF THE WORLD
SPEAK TO YOU OF SALVATION, WHICH I HAVE PURCHASED FOR YOU
PURCHASED WITH MY LIFE'S BLOOD, WHICH I GLADLY GAVE
YES, MY LITTLE ONES, YOUR KING OF KINGS, BECAME A SLAVE
I AM THE WORD THAT WAS IN THE BEGINNING, WHO TOOK ON FLESH
TO DESCEND TO EARTH, FROM HEAVEN, TO GIVE MY CHILDREN REST
MY YOUNG VIRGIN MOTHER, NOW QUEEN OF HEAVEN AND EARTH
LOVINGLY, GAVE HER WOMB, AS A SANCTUARY UNTIL MY BIRTH
WHEN THE TIME WAS FULFILLED YOUR LORD CAME INTO THE WORLD
NOURISHED BY MY BLESSED MOTHER, WITH LOVING ARMS UNFURLED
MY SERVANT, JOSEPH, PROTECTOR OF BLESSED MARY AND HER BABE
ACCEPTED HIS GOD AS HIS OWN SON, WHO IN THAT MANGER LAY

AS I GREW AND THE TIME WAS RIGHT, I STARTED MY MINISTRY
TO DO THE WORK OF SALVATION, WHICH MY FATHER ASSIGNED TO ME
TO SAVE THE WORLD FROM SIN AND DEATH, MYSELF, I WOULD DENY
FOR I WAS DESTINED, FOR ALL THE WORLD, TO BE RAISED UP ON HIGH
BUT FIRST, I CALLED ON MY SERVANTS, AND THEY DID NOT DISAGREE
FOR WHEN I CALLED, THEY LEFT ALL, TO COME AND FOLLOW ME
WE TRAVELLED FROM PLACE TO PLACE, MY KINGDOM TO PROCLAIM
SO ALL THE WORLD, COULD CLAIM SALVATION, IN MY MOST HOLY NAME
I TOLD ALL HOW THEY COULD FIND PEACE AND CHANGE THEIR FATE
TO LOVE THEIR GOD, AND LOVE EACH OTHER, TO ENTER HEAVEN'S GATE

I WAS REJECTED BY THE WORLD, JUST LIKE MY PROPHETS OF OLD
VERY FEW WERE THE WORKERS, AND MANY THE SEEDS TO SOW
THE SEEDS OF FAITH, AND HOPE AND TRUST IN THEIR SAVING LORD
FOR THEY MUST CONTINUE TO DO MY WORK AND BE OF ONE ACCORD
MANY THE SIGNS AND WONDERS, DID I PERFORM WITHIN THEIR SIGHT
AND MANY SINNERS TURNED TO ME, TO FOLLOW IN MY LIGHT
STILL, SOME WERE MISLED BY THE EVIL ONE, THE FATHER OF ALL LIES
HE EXISTS ONLY, FOR ONE PURPOSE, TO MAKE YOUR SOUL HIS PRIZE
THIS IS WHAT YOU MUST KNOW, MY CHILDREN, TREAD CAREFULLY
FOR IN ORDER TO COME TO THE FATHER, YOU MUST, FIRST, COME TO ME
LITTLE ONES, TO GAIN SALVATION, ADHERE NOT TO HATE AND SIN
I AM THE WAY, THE TRUTH AND THE LIFE, HEAVEN'S GATE; ENTER IN

LIVING TABERNACLE

OH, HUMBLE LITTLE VIRGIN MARY, SO PURE AND UNDEFILED
HOW OBEDIENT YOU WERE TO GOD, TO BEAR THE HOLY CHILD
FROM GOD A MESSAGE CAME TO YOU BY GABRIEL, SHINING BRIGHT
OH HOLY LIVING TABERNACLE, YOU WERE CHOSEN BY THE LIGHT
FOR GABRIEL SAID, 'HAIL FULL OF GRACE, THE LORD IS WITH THEE
IN YOUR WOMB, YOU SHALL CARRY THE SON OF GOD' SAID HE
YOU SPOKE AND SAID, "HOW CAN THIS BE, FOR I KNOW NOT MAN'
HOW COULD YOU, MOST HUMBLE BLESSED VIRGIN, UNDERSTAND
THEN GABRIEL SAID, 'THE HOLY SPIRIT SHALL COME UPON YOU,
AND THE POWER OF THE MOST HIGH WILL OVER SHADOW YOU.'
YOU REPLIED TO GABRIEL, 'BEHOLD I AM THE HANDMAID OF THE LORD,
MAY IT BE DONE TO ME, ACCORDING TO YOUR WORD'

THEN, BY THE MIGHTY POWER OF THE HOLY SPIRIT
OH MARY, EVER VIRGIN, YOU DID CONCEIVE
IN GOD, YOU PLACED YOUR TRUST; IN HIM, YOU DID BELIEVE
FOR THE LORD ALMIGHTY GOD'S HOLY WILL SHALL BE DONE
OH BLESSED MARY, LIVING TABERNACLE OF THE ANOINTED ONE
HE WHO IS CALLED JOSEPH, YOUR BETROTHED, A RIGHTEOUS MAN
WAS TROUBLED, FOR HE KNEW NOT OF OUR GOD'S HOLY PLAN
THE LORD SENT AN ANGEL TO HIM; FROM ALL DOUBTS SET HIM FREE
SAID HE, 'FEAR NOT, TAKE THY WIFE, MARY, INTO THY HOME WITH THEE
FOR SHE BEARS THE SON OF GOD, AND THEIR PROTECTOR, YOU SHALL BE
HE SHALL BE CALLED JESUS, THE MESSIAH, THE PROMISED ONE,
EMANUEL, GOD WITH US, GOD'S ONLY BEGOTTEN SON'

IMMACULATE MARY, SO FULL OF GRACE, FAVOURED BY GOD AND MAN
YOU WERE CONCEIVED WITHOUT SIN, PART OF THE DIVINE PLAN
YOU WERE CHOSEN BY THE LORD, TO BE HIS HOLY, BLESSED MOTHER
TO CARRY HIM BENEATH YOUR HEART, FOR HE WOULD HAVE NO OTHER
YOU PONDERED IN YOUR HEART THE THINGS THAT WERE TO COME
OH BLESSED, HOLY MOTHER OF GOD'S ONLY BEGOTTEN SON
YOU HUMBLY OBEYED OUR GOD'S WILL, TO SAVE THE SINFUL WORLD
FOR HE WOULD COME TO FREE US WITH SACRED ARMS UNFURLED
SO WE HONOR THEE, HOLY MARY, BY THY GRACE, WE ARE REDEEMED
OH HOLY BLESSED MOTHER, WHO GAVE BIRTH TO OUR SAVING KING
HE WAS BORN FOR US, A SAVIOR, THE WHOLE WORLD TO REDEEM
HOLY LIVING TABERNACLE, OUR ADVOCATE AND BLESSED QUEEN

IN YOUR MOST HOLY NAME

OH MOST SACRED HEART OF JESUS, PRECIOUS LORD OF ALL
WE COME WITH TRUSTING HEARTS, IN ANSWER TO YOUR CALL
FOR YOU HAVE OPENED YOUR SACRED ARMS TO ALL WHO BELIEVE
THAT WE MAY COME, IN FAITH, TO PROCLAIM OUR LOVE FOR THEE
TO THEE WE GIVE OUR PRAISE, MOST HOLY ONE WHOM WE ADORE
THAT YOU WILL REMEMBER US; BRING US THROUGH HEAVEN'S DOOR
LORD, WE ASK NOW THAT YOU MAY EVER, UPON US, POUR
ALL THAT WE MAY ASK OF YOU, NOW AND FOREVERMORE
FOR IT IS WRITTEN IN YOUR HOLY WORD, FOR ALL THE WORLD TO SEE
IF YOU SEEK REDEMPTION, CHILDREN, GIVE YOUR HEARTS TO ME
AND LORD YOU PROMISED, TO FREE US FROM ALL STRIFE AND PAIN
WHEN WE GATHER TOGETHER AND ASK IN YOUR MOST HOLY NAME

WE THANK YOU LORD FOR ALL THE BLESSINGS THAT YOU GIVE
FOR YOUR LIFE, DEATH AND RESURRECTION, SO THAT WE MIGHT LIVE
LORD, WE SEEK KNOWLEDGE, UNDERSTANDING, WISDOM AND GRACE
THAT WE MAY ALWAYS AND EVER SEEK YOUR HOLY BLESSED FACE
YOU HAVE INTERCEDED, FOR YOUR WAYWARD CHILDREN'S SAKE
AND THROUGH YOUR HOLY SACRIFICE, SATAN'S BONDS DID BREAK
LORD, LET US EVER REMAIN, IN A STATE OF HOLY GRACE
THAT, WHEN OUR LIVES ARE DONE, WE SHALL BEHOLD YOUR HOLY FACE
OUR IMMORTAL SOULS, LORD, YOU HOLD IN YOUR SACRED HANDS
WE PLACE OUR TRUST IN YOU, LORD, AS YOUR HOLY WORD COMMANDS
LORD KEEP US FREE FROM SIN, SO OUR SOULS REMAIN UNSTAINED
BLESSED SAVIOR, THIS, WE ASK IN YOUR MOST HOLY NAME

FOR THERE IS NO BETTER LOVE, THAT ANYONE CAN GIVE
THAN LAYING DOWN ONE'S LIFE, SO THAT OTHERS MAY LIVE
THIS YOU DID FOR US, AND MORE, HOLY LORD OF LOVE AND LIGHT
YOU RANSOMED YOUR CHILDREN; SAVED US FROM THE DARKEST NIGHT
TO YOU BE PRAISE FOREVER, OUR LORD, OUR SAVIOR, OUR KING
HOLY, HOLY, HOLY LORD, FOREVER WE SHALL SING
YOUR LOVE FOR US IS BOUNDLESS, YOU HAVE MADE US YOUR OWN
YOU SHED YOUR PRECIOUS BLOOD, TO BRING YOUR CHILDREN HOME
OH LORD OF ALL, KING OF GLORY, MOST HOLY ANOINTED ONE
YOU PAID THE COST TO SAVE THE LOST, GOD'S ONLY BEGOTTEN SON
YOU HAVE BOUGHT REDEMPTION FOR THE CHILDREN YOU NOW CLAIM,
MAY WE FOREVER LOVE AND TRUST, IN YOUR MOST HOLY NAME

MY CHOSEN MOTHER

CHILDREN, I MUST SAY THIS, YOU MUST REVERE MY HOLY MOTHER
SHE SHARED IN MY PLAN OF REDEMPTION, THERE COULD BE NO OTHER
FOR FROM THE BEGINNING, IT WAS PLANNED AND IT WAS ORDAINED
THAT MARY, INNOCENT MAIDEN, MY CHOSEN MOTHER, I WOULD CLAIM
SHE WAS BORN TO THE WORLD, WITHOUT THE STAIN OF ORIGINAL SIN
THAT, THROUGH HER, THE HOLY SPIRIT WOULD USHER REDEMPTION IN
STILL, YOUR LORD, GAVE HER THE CHANCE, TO SAY NO OR SAY YES
WITH LOVE AND TRUST, THIS HUMBLE MAID, SURELY PASSED THE TEST
SHE WAS A CHILD OF GRACE, WHO LOVED TO SERVE THE HOLY ONE
BEHOLD THE HANDMAID OF THE LORD, FOR GOD'S HOLY WILL BE DONE
FROM THIS HUMBLE VIRGIN, ALL MANKIND WOULD BE SAVED
A VIRGIN BIRTH, TO BRING FORTH, A KING WHO WOULD BE A SLAVE

CHILDREN, IT WAS ACCOMPLISHED. THROUGH THIS HOLY BLESSED ONE
THE WORD WOULD COME TO EARTH, GOD'S ONLY BEGOTTEN SON
THROUGH THE HOLY SPIRIT'S POWER AND THE WILL OF MY FATHER
BLESSED MARY, VIRGIN PURE, CONCEIVED A KING, THE LIVING WATER
FOR NOTHING SHALL BE IMPOSSIBLE WITH GOD, THE HOLY ONE
STILL A VIRGIN, SHE WAS TO BE THE MOTHER OF GOD'S ONLY SON
SHE NOURISHED ME, SHE BATHED ME, WITH A BLESSED MOTHER'S LOVE
THERE IS NO ONE, ON THE EARTH, OR IN THE HEAVENS ABOVE
THAT I LOVE MORE, THAN THIS HUMBLE VIRGIN WHO AGREED
DESPITE THE COMING SORROWS, TO BE A MOTHER TO ME
AS SPOKEN IN MY WORD, SHE SHALL BE BLESSED ABOVE ALL OTHERS
NOW SHE, QUEEN OF ANGELS, IS ALSO YOUR BLESSED MOTHER

UPON THE CROSS, BEFORE MY DEATH, MY FATHER'S WILL TO BE DONE
I SAID 'SON, BEHOLD THY MOTHER; WOMAN, BEHOLD THY SON'
TO MY FAITHFUL SERVANT JOHN, WHO IS SO SPECIAL TO ME
I GAVE UNTO HIM, MY MOTHER, AND I ALSO GAVE TO THEE
MY MOTHER, TO HELP THEE ALONG THE WAY, TO FOLLOW ON THE PATH
OF HOLY REDEMPTION, TO SPARE YOU, MY CHILDREN, FROM THE WRATH
FOR YOU, SHE PRAYS ALWAYS, SO THAT WITH ME YOU SHALL HAVE LIFE
TO SAVE YOU FROM THE DARKNESS, TO BRING YOU INTO MY HOLY LIGHT
SO, MY CHILDREN, FEAR NOT, TO PRAY TO HER TO INTERCEDE FOR THEE
AS I INTERCEDE WITH MY FATHER, TO BLESS YOU ABUNDANTLY
FOR WHO IN HEAVAEN OR ON EARTH; BESIDES GOD, THERE IS NO OTHER
WHO CAN INTERCEDE WITH HER SON, FOR SHE IS MY CHOSEN MOTHER

ROYAL PRIEST

JESUS CHRIST OUR LORD AND GOD, ROYAL PRIEST FOR ALL TIME
WE GIVE YOU ALL PRAISE, HONOR AND GLORY, OH LOVE DIVINE
YOU ESTABLISHED YOUR KINGDOM WHEN YOU TOOK ON OUR FLESH
YOU CAME TO SHOW US THE WAY, TO FIND ETERNAL REST
YOU PAID THE RANSOM PRICE, OH MOST HOLY SACRIFICE
WHAT COULD BE MORE PERFECT THAN OUR GOD, ETERNAL LIGHT
THERE IS NOTHING WE CAN DO TO SAVE OUR IMMORTAL SOULS
ONLY YOU, LORD, COULD SAVE US, ONLY YOU COULD MAKE US WHOLE
BY YOUR PRECIOUS, SAVING BLOOD, YOU WON THE VICTORY
YOU DEFEATED DEATH AND SIN, PRECIOUS LAMB WHO SETS US FREE
FOR THIS WE GIVE YOU THANKS AND PRAISE, OH HOLY IMMORTAL ONE
THANK YOU HEAVENLY FATHER, YOU SENT YOUR ONLY SON

TRIUMPHANTLY, YOU ROSE TO GLORY ON THAT HOLY THIRD DAY
THOUGH THEY LAY YOU IN THE TOMB; THERE YOU DID NOT STAY
GOD HAS RAISED YOU FROM THE DEAD, OH PRAISE YOUR HOLY HAME
THEY HAD TRIED TO DESTROY YOU, BUT BACK TO LIFE YOU CAME
FOR YOU ARE GOD, THE ONE HIGH PRIEST, THE KEY TO HEAVEN'S DOOR
JESUS, SON OF GOD AND MAN, IT IS YOU WHOM WE ADORE
BY YOUR DEATH, MERCIFUL LORD, YOU SET THE CAPTIVES FREE
YOU SET YOUR FACE LIKE FLINT, NEVER UTTERING A PLEA
THEY WRAPPED YOU IN A SCARLET ROBE AND MOCKED YOU AS A KING
IN MY MIND AND HEART I HEAR THE DREADFUL HAMMERING
AS SINNERS NAILED YOU TO THE CROSS, OH HOLY WORD, SO TRUE
YOU PRAYED, 'FORGIVE THEM FATHER; THEY KNOW NOT WHAT THEY DO'

JESUS, LORD OF ALL, TRUE LIVING BREAD OF REDEMPTION
OH MOST HIGH ETERNAL PRIEST, YOUR LOVE BOUGHT US SALVATION
YOU ARE THE GOD OF ISRAEL, THE BEGINNING AND THE END
THE LORD MOST HIGH, OUR SAVIOR, OUR BROTHER AND OUR FRIEND
FOREVER YOU SHALL BE THE HIGH PRIEST OF OUR FAITH
AND YOU SHALL EVER BLESS YOUR CHILDREN WHO AWAIT
FAITHFULLY, AND WITH HOPE AND TRUST, FOR YOU TO RETURN
TO SEE YOU COME IN GLORIOUS TRIUMPH, IT IS FOR THIS, WE YEARN
YOU SHALL CLAIM THOSE, WHOM YOU HAVE, BY YOUR BLOOD REDEEMED
AND YOU SHALL RULE FOREVERMORE, ROYAL PRIEST, AND HEAVENLY KING
OH LORD, MAY WE BE READY, TO ENTER HEAVEN'S GOLDEN DOOR
WHERE WE SHALL PRAISE WITH HANDS UPRAISED, OUR GOD, FOREVERMORE

ROSES OF LOVE

OH MARY, QUEEN OF VIRGINS, QUEEN OF ANGELS, SAINTS AND MAN
TO THEE, I TURN FOR INTERCESSION, EXTEND THY BLESSED HANDS
FOR WE ARE BOUND TO YOU, BLESSED OF GOD, LIKE NO OTHER
WE GIVE TO YOU, THIS DAY, ROSES OF LOVE, DEAR VIRGIN MOTHER
WE SHALL BOW TO YOUR WISHES AND PRAY THE ROSARY
WHICH IS LIKE A BOUQUET OF ROSES, DEAR BLESSED MOTHER, TO THEE

FOR YOU HAVE SAID, THE ROSARY CAN SAVE ALL OF MANKIND
INTERCEDE FOR ALL SINNERS, THOSE WITH EYES THAT ARE BLIND
TO THE WAY, THE TRUTH AND THE LIFE, YOUR HOLY BLESSED SON
AND TURN THEM TO ALMIGHTY GOD, THE HOLY IMMORTAL ONE
SO EACH PRAYER, ON EACH BEAD, IS A BEAUTIFUL LIVING ROSE
SENT TO YOU, OUR BLESSED MOTHER, WHOM OUR GOD CHOSE

FOR YOUR SON, OUR SAVIOR, SAID, 'NEGLECT NOT MY PRECIOUS MOTHER
FOR THROUGH HER IS SAVED MANY SOULS, TRULY THERE IS NO OTHER
MORE BLESSED BY GOD, TO INTERCEDE WITH HIS HOLY SON, FOR YOU
WHO PRAYS CONSTANTLY, FOR HER CHILDREN, FOR HER LOVE IS TRUE
IF WE PRAY THE ROSARY, AS YOU, DEAR MOTHER DO REQUEST,
WE ARE YOUR SONS AND DAUGHTERS, BROTHERS AND SISTERS OF JESUS

AS FOR ME, I SHALL BE HAPPY TO PRAY THE BEAUTIFUL ROSARY
WHICH IS SENDING A BOUQUET OF ROSES, BLESSED MOTHER, TO THEE
AND WITH EACH DECADE OF ROSES, WE ARE PERMITTED TO REQUEST
BLESSINGS FOR OURSELVES, AND BLESSINGS FOR THE REST
OH HEAVENLY QUEEN OF ANGELS, OF SAINTS, AND OF MAN
PLEASE ACCEPT THESE ROSES OF LOVE, IN KEEPING WITH GOD'S PLAN

MOST DIVINE PHYSICIAN

OH JESUS, DIVINE PHYSICIAN, WHO KNOWS OUR ILLNESS
KNOWS OUR WEAKNESS, OUR FRAILITIES AND OUR PAIN
GOD OF LOVE, BORN TO SUFFER FOR THE SINS OF MAN
OH MOST HOLY SON OF THE FATHER, EXTEND YOUR BLESSED HANDS
TOUCH YOUR SERVANT, WHO LONGS FOR HEALING, IF IT BE THY WILL
YOU ARE THE PRECIOUS LAMB OF GOD, WHO DIED ON CALVARY HILL
YOU CAME TO SAVE THE CAPTIVES, BOUND BY DEATH AND SIN
YOU OPENED THE DOORS TO HEAVEN, BID YOUR CHILDREN TO ENTER IN
OH MOST HOLY, DIVINE PHYSICAIN, YOU HAVE NO NEED FOR A DEGREE
FOR WHO CAN MAKE ME WELL, LIKE HE WHO CREATED ME
YOU BREATHED YOUR SPIRIT WITHIN ME, LORD, CREATOR DIVINE
YOU NEED BUT WILL IT TO BE, LORD, AND HEALING WILL BE MINE

OH LORD, I IMPLORE THEE, LIGHTEN THE BURDENS OF MY SOUL
FOR ONLY YOU CAN HEAL ME, ONLY YOU CAN MAKE ME WHOLE
LORD I LOVE THEE WITH ALL MY HEART, I OFFER MY ALL TO THEE
YOU CAME FOR THE CHILDREN YOU LOVE, YOU CAME TO SET US FREE
LORD, YOU HAVE SUFFERED FOR US ALL, EVEN UNTO DEATH
RESTORE ME TO HEALTH, MY SAVOR, IN YOUR LOVING KINDNESS
YOUR BOUNDLESS LOVE, CONSOLATION AND EVERLASTING MERCY
SHALL MOVE YOU, MOST DIVINE PHYSICIAN, TO HEAL MY INFIRMITIES
AND I SHALL SERVE YOU FERVANTLY, FOR THE REST OF MY DAYS
EVEN IF I AM HEALED NOT, FROM YOU, I SHALL NOT STRAY
IN YOU, I SHALL FIND COURAGE AND STRENGTH THAT I SHALL NEED
TO SERVE MY GOD, WHO DIED FOR US, TO SET THE CAPTIVES FREE

IF IT SO PLEASE, THE FATHER, IF IT SO PLEASE THE SON,
THROUGH THE POWER OF YOUR HOLY SPIRIT, LORD, LET IT BE DONE
HEAL ME LORD, IN SPIRIT, RELEASE ME FROM ALL PAIN
YOU WHO SHOW YOUR LOVING MERCY, AGAIN AND AGAIN
YOU SHOWED ME HOW TO FORGIVE THOSE WHO HAVE HURT ME
FROM ALL THOSE PAST HURTS IN MY LIFE, YOU HAVE SET ME FREE
NOW I ASK LORD, IN YOUR HOLY NAME, LET NOT THE ENEMY WIN
HE WANTS ME NOT TO BE WITH YOU, LET HIM NOT ENTER IN
LET HIM NOT KEEP ME FROM YOU; IN YOUR GRACE, PERMIT ME TO STAY
HE IS EVER TRYING, TO MAKE ME TURN FROM THY WAYS
WITH ILLNESS THAT LEAVES ME HELPLES; IT TAKES MY VERY BREATH
MOST DIVINE PHYSICIAN, HEAL ME, FOR WITH YOU, THERE IS NO DEATH

MOTHER OF SORROWS

OH BLESSED MOTHER OF GOD, QUEEN OF ANGELS AND SAINTS
HOW YOUR BLESSED HEART MUST HAVE BEEN PIERCED
TO SEE THY BELOVED SON, GOING QUIETLY TO HIS DEATH
YOUR HEAD BOWED DOWN IN SORROW, AS HE DREW IN HIS LAST BREATH
THEY BEAT HIM, AND MOCKED HIM AND CROWNED HIM WITH THORNS
HOW COULD YOU BEAR IT, HOW YOUR HEART MUST HAVE TORN
WITH SORROW AS YOU WATCHED YOUR BLESSED HOLY SON,
THE SON OF THE MOST HIGH GOD, HIS ONLY BEGOTTEN ONE
FULFILLING THE PROMISE MADE BY GOD IN THOSE DAYS OF OLD
HE HUMBLY BORE THE HEAVY CROSS, TO SAVE OUR SINFUL SOULS
HE HAD NOT SINNED, NOR BROKE A LAW, NOR CAUSED ANYONE HARM
STILL, HE SILENTLY BORE THE SHAME, AND STRETCHED OUT HIS ARMS

HOLY MOTHER OF SORROWS, THESE THINGS YOU HAD TO SEE
MY PRECIOUS LORD WHO SHED HIS BLOOD, TO SAVE A WRETCH LIKE ME
STILL, YOU PRAY FOR THE WHOLE WORLD, THE FATHER TO FORGIVE
THOUGH IT WAS YOUR PRECIOUS SON, WHO DIED SO I COULD LIVE
MOTHER OF SORROWS, BLESSED ONE, I SHALL FOREVER PRAY
IN THANKFULNESS, TO MY SAVING GOD, FOR WHAT HE DID THAT DAY
AND I SHALL, ALWAYS AND EVER, MY HOLY MOTHER, VENERATE
WHO TEARFULLY WATCHED HER HOLY SON TREATED WITH SUCH HATE
HOLY MOTHER OF SORROWS, HOW HURT YOU MUST HAVE BEEN
TO SEE OUR BLESSED SAVIOR, INNOCENT LAMB, WITHOUT SIN
SUFFER OUR HUMILIATIONS, TO ANSWER THE FATHER'S CALL
AND DYING, DEAR MARY, HE GAVE YOU, AS MOTHER TO US ALL

REMEMBER, HOLY MARY, THOUGH SORROWFUL WAS THAT DAY
HE WAS TO RISE UP FROM THE DEAD, TO WASH OUR SINS AWAY
THE THIRD DAY, THEY FIND AN OPEN TOMB; JESUS WAS NOT WITHIN
HE WHO SHED HIS PRECIOUS BLOOD, SURELY LIVES AGAIN
HOLY MOTHER OF SORROWS, YOUR SORROWS TURNED TO JOY
AS YOU BEHELD YOUR BELOVED SON, WHO WAS YOUR BABY BOY
HE APPEARED TO HIS FOLLOWERS, AND TO YOU, HIS BLESSED MOTHER
THERE IS NO GOD LIKE OUR GOD; INDEED THERE IS NO OTHER
HE CONQUERED SIN, HE CONQUERED DEATH, AND HE FOREVER REIGNS
FOR HE IS OUR SAVING LORD, WHO DIED AND ROSE AGAIN
WE SHALL PRAISE HIS HOLY NAME, OUR HANDS RAISED TO HEAVEN
BECAUSE OF THIS PRECIOUS, HOLY LAMB, OUR SINS ARE FORGIVEN

RENEW US LORD

LORD JESUS CHRIST, REDEEMING LORD, AND HOLY LIGHT
RENEW US WHO COME TO PRAISE THY HOLY NAME TONIGHT
WITH DEEP DEVOTION AND FERVANT PRAYER, LORD WE COME TO YOU
THAT YOU MAY, RENEW OUR SOULS, AND MAKE OUR HEARTS ANEW
LORD, YOU DIED AND ROSE AGAIN, FOR YOUR CHILDREN'S SALVATION
FOR WHOEVER IS IN CHRIST, HAS BECOME A NEW CREATION
RENEW US LORD, AND HEAL US WITH YOUR EVERLASTING LOVE
LET YOUR SPIRIT REST UPON US, IN THE LIKENESS OF A DOVE
AS HE DID LITE UPON YOU, WHEN JOHN HAD BAPTIZED THEE
GOD SPOKE "THIS IS MY BELOVED SON, IN WHOM I AM WELL PLEASED"
BEHOLD, YOUR CHILDREN, LORD, WITH LOVE AND COMPASSION
RENEW OUR HOPE, DISPEL OUR FEARS, LET NOT SIN BE A DISTRACTION

OH HOLY IMMORTAL GOD, WHO DIED FOR OUR SALVATION
HIDE YOUR CHILDREN NEATH YOUR WINGS, OH GOD OF ALL CREATION
RENEW OUR LOVE, RENEW OUR FAITH, RENEW OUR TRUST IN YOU
RENEW OUR STRENGTH, RENEW OUR PEACE, LET US BE EVER TRUE
TO OUR ONE AND ONLY GOD, MAY WE FIND JOY AND PEACE
WE SERVE AN AWESOME, MIGHTY KING, HIS LOVE WILL NEVER CEASE
NO MATTER HOW WE OFFEND YOU, OUR LORD OF LOVE AND LIGHT
YOU ARE EVER WILLING TO FORGIVE, YOU KINDLY MAKE THINGS RIGHT
GIVER OF LIFE, GIVER OF LOVE, GIVER OF HOPE AND SALVATION
YOU SHALL COME BACK, OH HOLY LORD, TO JUDGE EVERY NATION
REMEMBER US, REDEEMING LORD, HOLY IS YOUR NAME
IN YOUR MOST TENDER MERCY LORD, RENEW US ONCE AGAIN.

ETERNAL FATHER, I THANK YOU

ETERNAL FATHER, I THANK YOU FOR ALL THY INFINITE GOODNESS
THROUGH YOUR UNENDING LOVE, YOU SENT YOUR HOLY SPIRIT UPON ME
MAY HE, THROUGH HIS UNDERSTANDING, ENLIGHTEN MY DARKNESS
MAY HE FOREVER TAKE FULL POSSESSION OF ALL I MAY EVER BE
MAY HE LIVE FOREVER IN MY HEART, AND OVER IT, TAKE REIGN
SO THAT I MAY CHOOSE TO FOREVER PRAISE YOUR MOST HOLY NAME
MAY HE FILL ME WITH POWERFUL LIGHT TO KEEP ME FROM DARKNESS
AND THROUGH, HIS MIGHTY POWER, MAY HE HEAL ALL MY ILLNESS
MAY HE AWAYS GUIDE ME BY HIS MOST POWERFUL COUNSEL
AND WITH HIS DIVINE KNOWLEDGE, MAY HE INSTRUCT ME WELL
MAY HE GRANT ME, THE GIFT OF PIETY, THAT I MAY FERVANTLY PRAY
AND MAY HE GRANT ME DIVINE FEAR, TO KEEP ALL EVIL AWAY

MAY HE GRANT ME GIFTS AND GRACES TO CAUSE MY FACE TO SHINE
MAY HE DRIVE OUT ALL THAT MAY DEFILE MY SOUL, OH GOD DIVINE
MAY HE GRANT ME THE GIFTS OF KNOWLEDGE, UNDERSTANDING, PIETY
FORTITUDE AND WISDOM, COUNSEL, ETERNAL FATHER LET IT BE
HOLY, ALMIGHTY GOD, THANK YOU FOR ALL YOU HAVE DONE FOR ME
YOU SENT YOUR BLESSED SON, BORN OF FLESH, TO SET ME FREE
MAY I BE FILLED WITH HOLY FEAR, AND WORSHIP THE HOLY ONE
WHO WILLINGLY DIED UPON THE CROSS, YOUR ONLY BEGOTTEN SON
AND MAY YOUR HOLY SPIRIT EVER AND ALWAYS INSPIRE ME TO WRITE
LET MY PEN, LORD, BE YOUR SWORD, THE EVIL ONE, TO FIGHT
NOT WITH WORDS OF DAMNATION, NOR JUDGEMENT, BUT OF PEACE
UNTIL, AT LAST, YOU CALL ME HOME, MY BURDENS TO RELEASE

THANK YOU ETERNAL FATHER, FOR GRANTING ME YOUR HOLY GRACE
FOR GIVING ME FAITH AND HOPE THAT I MAY SEE YOUR BLESSED FACE
MAY I FOREVER SERVE, MY LORD, MY MASTER AND MY KING
ALWAYS AND FOREVER WITH JOYOUS SONG, YOUR PRAISES SING
YOU ARE OUR SAVING LORD, FOR YOU HAVE SENT YOUR ONLY SON
WHO DIED AND ROSE TO GLORY, PRAISE TO YOU, OH HOLY ONE
GLORIOUSLY ALIVE, APPEARING TO HIS MOTHER AND HIS FRIENDS
SO THEY MAY SPREAD HIS HOLY WORDS, OF HIS LOVE WITHOUT END
HIS TEACHINGS SHALL LIVE FOREVER, IMPRINTED ON OUR HEARTS
TO SAVE US ALL FROM DARKNESS, FROM HIM WE SHALL NOT PART
THANK YOU ETERNAL FATHER, FOR SENDING US SALVATION
YOUR WORD SHALL BE PROCLAIMED TO ALL, TO EACH AND EVERY NATION

HOLY SPIRIT OF GOD

HOLY SPIRIT OF GOD, YOU ARE WORSHIPPED AND GLORIFIED
FOR YOU ARE ONE WITH THE FATHER AND THE SON WHO, FOR ME, DIED
AND WHO, WITH MIGHTY POWER, MADE VIRGIN MARY, MOTHER OF GOD
YOU GIVE HOPE AND CONSOLATION, MY COUNSELOR AND MY GUIDE
COME, OH HOLY SPIRIT, BE FOREVER BY MY SIDE
MY COMFORTER AND MY GOD, YOU TEACH, AND SANCTIFY
HOLY, HOLY, IMMORTAL GOD, WHO LIFTS ME WHEN I FALL
YOU ARE MY HELPER, MY EDUCATOR, FOR MY GOD KNOWS ALL
YOU WHO INTERCEDE FOR ME, WITH THE FATHER AND THE SON
YOU ARE EVER WITHIN ME, MIGHTY SPIRIT OF THE HOLY ONE
THROUGH YOUR MIGHTY POWER, CHRIST OUR LORD WAS BORN
MIGHTY KING, AND SAVING LORD, CROWNED WITH PEIRCING THORNS

HOLY SPIRIT, YOU ARE MY COMFORT, WHEN LIFE IS FILLED WITH PAIN
YOU COME AND YOU CONSOLE ME, OH PRAISE GOD'S HOLY NAME
I GIVE TO YOU THIS DAY, ALL OF MY FEARS, MY HOPES, MY DREAMS
WITH THE FATHER AND THE SON, YOU ARE MY EVERYTHING
HOLY, MIGHTY, IMMORTAL GOD, WHO WANTS TO SET ME FREE
BECAUSE I NEEDED A SAVIOR, YOU SENT YOUR SON TO ME
COME OH HOLY SPIRIT, EVER LIVE IN MY MIND AND HEART
SO THAT FROM MY SAVING LORD, I SHALL NEVER BE APART
YOU GENTLY REMIND ME, WHEN I SHOULD KNEEL AND PRAY
SO THE WHOLE WORLD SHOULD TURN TO GOD IN EACH AND EVERY WAY
WHEN MY LIFE ON EARTH IS COMPLETE, MY WORK FOR MY GOD DONE
MAY YOU COME TO GUIDE ME HOME, OH HOLY IMMORTAL ONE

IN GOD'S HEAVENLY GARDEN

HAPPY ARE THOSE WHO DWELL WITH GOD; FIND ETERNAL LOVE
DELIGHTFUL ARE THE REWARDS, AS THEY COME INTO THE LIGHT
THEY SHALL HAVE ETERNAL LOVE, JOY, PEACE AND HAPPINESS
THOSE WHO CHOOSE THEIR SAVING GOD, SHALL LIVE IN HOLY BLISS
LIVE YOUR LIFE FOR JESUS, IF YOU SIN, YOU MUST SEEK PARDON
THEN, AND ONLY THEN, SHALL YOU ENTER HIS HEAVENLY GARDEN
WHERE YOU SHALL BE PERMITTED TO EAT OF THE TREE OF KNOWLEDGE
OF THINGS MYSTERIOUSLY HIDDEN, YOU SHALL THEN BE PRIVLEGED
WITH KNOWLEDGE COMES UNDERSTANDING OF THE BLESSED TRINITY
OBEY THE LORD, AND THIS SHALL BE YOURS, FOR ALL ETERNITY
FOR ALL WHO KNOCK, THE DOOR WILL BE OPENED, ALL WHO SEEK SHALL FIND
ASK; IT SHALL BE GIVEN UNTO YOU, YOU SHALL NO LONGER BE BLIND

MY CHILDREN, YOU MUST PRAISE YOUR SAVIOR'S MOST HOLY NAME
FOR YOU, I BORE THE CROSS AND FOR YOUR SINS I TOOK THE BLAME
OBEY MY WORDS, LOVE YOUR NEIGHBOR, BUT GOD, ABOVE ALL OTHERS
HAVE REVERENCE FOR THE BLESSED VIRGIN, MY MOST HOLY MOTHER
HARM NOT YOUR FELLOW MAN, BUT BLESS HIM IN MY HOLY NAME
I RETURN TO BURN THE CHAFF, IN THE EVERLASTING FLAMES
BUT THE GOOD GRAIN, I SHALL GATHER, AND I SHALL TAKE WITH ME
HOME TO MY HEAVENLY FATHER, WHERE WONDERS YOU SHALL SEE
TAKE CARE TO STAY IN MY HOLY GRACE, BE OF GOOD HARVEST
IF YOU SHOULD SIN, HAVE SORROW, I FORGIVE THOSE WHO CONFESS
I SHALL GIVE YOU ABUNDANT LOVE, AND YOU SHALL LIVE ETERNALLY
FOR ALL WHO LIVE IN MY HOLY LIGHT, ARE THOSE I SHALL SET FREE

WHEN YOU COME UNTO THE LORD, PRAISE HIS MOST HOLY NAME
FOR YOU HE SUFFERED, FOR YOU, HE DIED AND FOR YOU HE ROSE AGAIN
YOU MUST LOVE AND ADORE HIM; AND IN HIS GRACE STRIVE TO STAY
SEEK ALWAYS TO OBEY HIS HOLY WORD; ALWAYS AND EVER PRAY
FOR PROTECTION FROM THE DECEIVER WHO TEMPTS YOU INTO SIN
TO CLAIM YOUR IMMORTAL SOUL; IN MY NAME YOU SHALL BANISH HIM
CLING UNTO ME, YOUR SAVIOR, IN MY LIGHT, ENDEAVOR TO LIVE
I AM THE LIGHT OF THE WORLD, YOUR INIQUITIES, I SHALL FORGIVE
WHEN IT IS TIME TO ENTER MY KINGDOM, IT IS, I, YOU SHALL MEET
AND I SHALL REVEAL MY WOUNDS, TO MY HANDS, MY SIDE, MY FEET
I SHALL SHOW YOU GOD'S HEAVENLY GARDEN, WHEREIN YOU SHALL SEE
THE TREE OF LIFE, FROM WHICH YOU SHALL EAT, TO LIVE ETERNALLY

THE POWER OF PRAYER

MY CHILDREN, DO NOT UNDER ESTIMATE THE POWER OF PRAYER
IF YOU WISH TO DWELL IN PARADISE, PRAYER SHALL GET YOU THERE
HE OR SHE WHO CONSTANTLY PRAYS, AND INVOKES MY HOLY NAME
SHALL NOT SUFFER DAMNATION, SHALL NOT BE PUT TO THE FLAMES
TAKE TIME TO PRAY, AS MUCH AS YOU CAN, NOT TO SUFFER THE SWORD
THE MORE YOU PRAY, IN SPIRIT, THE CLOSER TO THE LORD
PRAY, NOT ONLY FOR YOURSELVES, BUT PRAY FOR THE WHOLE WORLD
AND PRAY TO MY HOLY SPIRIT, WHO COMES WITH WINGS UNFURLED
MY CHILDREN, BELIEVE ME WHEN I SAY HOW IMPORTANT IT IS TO PRAY
FOR ONLY PRAYER, CAN SAVE YOU, BELOVED, LISTEN TO WHAT I SAY
WITHOUT EARNEST PRAYER, HOW CAN MY CHILDREN RECEIVE
ALL THAT YOUR GOD, WANTS TO GIVE TO ALL THOSE WHO BELIEVE

MANY THE GIFTS, I, THE LORD, HAVE FOR YOU, IF YOU ONLY ASK
I SHALL GIVE ABUNDANTLY TO THOSE WHO CHOOSE THE TASK
TO WORK FOR THE SALVATION OF SOULS, NOT ONLY FOR YOUR OWN
FOR I WISH ALL MY CHILDREN TO WORSHIP AT MY THRONE
YOU MUST BE BORN AGAIN, INTO THE LIGHT OF MY HOLY SPIRIT
LET THOSE WITH EYES, PERCEIVE, LET THOSE WITH EARS, HEAR IT
ALWAYS AND EVER PRAY TO YOUR LORD, FOR PRAYER IS THE ONLY WAY
TO SAVE YOUR IMMORTAL SOULS; FROM GOD, TO NEVER STRAY
MY CHILDREN, THE KINGDOM OF HEAVEN, IS THE HOLY PLACE WHERE
YOU SHALL GAIN ETERNAL JOY, JUST USE THE POWER OF PRAYER

OBEY MY WORD

MY CHILDREN, I DESIRE THAT YOU SPREAD THESE WORDS,
I, THE LORD, SAY THAT IF YOU WANT ETERNAL HAPPINESS
OBEY MY WORD, MY COMMANDMENTS, YOU MUST OBSERVE
LET MY HOLY SPIRIT, DWELL IN YOU, TO HAVE ETERNAL REST
MY CHILDREN, THE TIME APPROACHES, FOR YOUR LORD'S RETURN
WHEN SATAN AND HIS COHORTS SHALL BE CAST OUT FOREVER
HE IS HARD AT WORK; TO STEAL YOUR SOULS, HE YEARNS
IF YOU TURN TO ME, YOUR REDEEMER, I WILL FORSAKE YOU NEVER
REPENT OF YOUR SINS, AND YOU SHALL FOREVER DWELL WITH ME
IF YOU TURN TO THE ONE TRUE GOD, IN DARKNESS YOU SHALL NOT BE
COME INTO MY HOLY LIGHT, AND YOU SHALL HAVE ETERNAL LIFE
WHERE YOU SHALL BE FREE OF ALL SORROW, ALL PAIN AND ALL STRIFE

OBEY MY WORDS OF SALVATION, RETURN TO YOUR SAVIOR, YOUR LORD
YOU SHALL NOT FACE ETERNAL FIRE, NOR SUFFER THE REAPER'S SWORD
LOVE YOUR GOD, WITH ALL YOUR HEART, CLAIM JESUS FOR YOUR OWN
MY CHILDREN, DO GOOD, NOT EVIL, AND I SHALL SURELY BRING YOU HOME
WHERE I SHALL BE YOUR GOD, AND YOU SHALL BE MY PEOPLE
LET NOT SATAN, DECEIVE YOU; WITH HIM, THERE IS NO LIGHT
I AM YOUR GOD ALMIGHTY, ALL LOVING, ALL POWERFUL ALL MERCIFUL
SATAN, THE DECEIVER, CAN BRING YOU ONLY, THE DARK NIGHT
HE WANTS YOU TO THINK, THAT WITH HIM, YOU SHALL HAVE GREAT POWER
MY CHILDREN, BELIEVE HIM NOT, FOR SOON SHALL COME THE HOUR
WHEN YOUR SAVIOR RETURNS AT LAST TO JUDGE THE LIVING AND THE DEAD
WITH SATAN YOU HAVE ONLY DARKNESS, CHOOSE THE LIVING WORD INSTEAD

CHOOSE THE ONE, WHO DIED FOR YOU, TO SAVE YOU FROM YOUR SINS
YOU MUST REPENT, CLAIM YOUR REDEEMER, AND, ONLY HIM, ADORE
JESUS, THE CHRIST, YOUR SAVIOR, IN HIM ONLY CAN YOU ENTER IN
THE HOLY KINGDOM OF THE LORD, WHERE ETERNAL LIFE SHALL BE YOURS
FOR GOD THE ALMIGHTY IS LOVE, AND GOD'S LOVE IS TRUE LIGHT
THINK, MY LITTLE ONES, YOU COULD HAVE ETERNAL SALVATION
SATAN IS ONLY DARKNESS, HORROR, SUFFERING AND BLIGHT
IF HIM, YOU CHOOSE, YOU SHALL SUFFER ETERNAL DAMNATION
REMEMBER, MY CHILDREN, THE LOVE OF YOUR LORD IS TRUE
I CHOSE DEATH ON THE CROSS, IN ORDER TO RANSOM YOU
CHOOSE THE LIGHT, MY CHILDREN, COME TO THE FIRE OF THE SPIRIT
THE DECEIVER, HOLDS ETERNAL PAIN, LET THOSE WITH EARS, HEAR IT

THE TIME SHALL COME

MY CHILDREN, THE TIME SHALL COME FOR THE FAITHFUL TO BE STRONG
THE DECEIVER, WHO RULES THE EARTH, CAUSING HAVOC, HAS NOT LONG
FOR YOUR GOD SHALL MARK THE PERFECT MAN, AND BEHOLD THE UPRIGHT
THOSE CHILDREN WHO LOVE THEIR GOD, SHALL NOT SUFFER THE DARK NIGHT
I SHALL COME MOUNTED ON A POWERFUL STEED WITH FIRE IN HIS BREATH
TO THOSE WHO ARE IN THE SPIRIT, BE FAITHFUL UNTO DEATH
YOUR LORD COMETH, AND TO THE FIERY PIT; THE EVIL ONE HE SHALL SEND
I AM ALPHA AND OMEGA, THE FIRST AND LAST, THE BEGINNING AND THE END

BE NOT OVERCOME OF EVIL, BUT OVERCOME EVIL, WITH GOOD
THEREFORE, IF THINE ENEMY HUNGER, FEED HIM, AS YOU SHOULD
IF HE THIRST, GIVE HIM DRINK, FOR IN SO DOING THOU SHALT HEAP
BURNING COALS OF FIRE ON HIS HEAD, AND HE SHALL SOON WEEP
BECAUSE HE KNOWS NOT WHY, THE ENEMY WOULD TREAT HIM WELL
IF HE SHOULD CHOOSE TO LISTEN, MY CHILDREN, FEAR NOT TO TELL,
PRIDE GOETH BEFORE DESTRUCTION; A HAUGHTY SPIRIT BEFORE A FALL
FOR HE MAY TURN TO THE SAVING LORD, AND REPENT, FOR I FORGIVE ALL

IF ONE IS NOT IN THE GRACE OF GOD, BUT REPENT OF HIS SINS
IF WITH SORROWFUL HEART, HE CALLS ON ME, I SHALL RECEIVE HIM AGAIN
FOR WHAT IS A MAN PROFITED, IF HE SHALL GAIN THE WHOLE WORLD
BUT LOSE HIS OWN SOUL, SO I SHALL GREET HIM WITH ARMS UNFURLED
SOME MIGHT SAY, WHY HAVE YOU TREATED HIM THUS, HE HAS AN EVIL HEART
THEN, I SHALL SAY, LET HIM WITHOUT SIN, CAST THE FIRST STONE; OR DEPART
FOR MY CHILDREN, YOU, WHO ARE ALREADY BLESSED, AND IN MY GRACE
IF YOUR BROTHER, WHO WAS LOST, RETURNS, SHALL YOU TURN YOUR FACE

MY CHILDREN, PROVE ALL THINGS; THAT WHICH IS GOOD, HOLD FAST
TREAT YOUR ENEMIES WITH KINDNESS, CAUSE NO ONE NEEDLESS STRIFE
BLESSED IS THE MAN THAT ENDURES TEMPTATION FOR WHEN HE IS TRIED
IF THERE IS FOUND NO EVIL IN HIM, HE SHALL RECEIVE THE CROWN OF LIFE
BE WATCHFUL, MY CHILDREN, AND FROM YOUR LORD, DO NOT GO ASTRAY
FOR ONLY THE ALMIGHTY FATHER KNOWS THE NIGHT OR DAY
WHEN THE ANOINTED ONE SHALL RETURN, AND HE SHALL AT LAST
BRING HIS BELOVED TO THEIR REWARD; THE WICKED, INTO THE FIRE, CAST

(Part of this poem is put together with many famous bible quotes)
(I thank the Lord for leading me in this endeavor)

LOVE'S PURE LIGHT

MY CHILDREN, I AM ABOUT TO REVEAL TO YOU
SOMETHING THAT YOU MUST BELIEVE IS TRUE
FOR YOU ARE MY CHILDREN, YOU ARE SO SPECIAL TO ME
THAT TO HEAVEN'S DOOR, YOU SHALL FIND THE KEY
BECAUSE, IN YOU, MY CHILDREN, I DELIGHT
I SHALL TELL YOU ALL ABOUT LOVE'S PURE LIGHT
FIRST, YOU MUST KNOW, THAT YOUR GOD IS LOVE
AND THAT HE IS ENTHRONED IN HEAVEN ABOVE
GOD IS LOVE, MY CHILDREN, AND LOVE IS LIGHT
YOU SHALL BEHOLD HIS PRESENCE SHINING BRIGHT
KNOW THAT JESUS, THE MESSIAH, IS LOVE SO PURE
THAT HE IS THE LIGHT OF THE WORLD FOREVERMORE

CHILDREN, YOU ARE PART OF THE MYSTICAL BODY OF CHRIST
AND CHRIST IS LOVE, MY CHILDREN, AND LOVE IS LIGHT
SO SHALL YOU, MY LITTLE ONES, THIS LIGHT INHEIRIT
YOU ARE ONE WITH THE FATHER, THE SON; THE HOLY SPIRIT
LISTEN, MY CHILDREN, AS THIS REVELATION, I TELL
YOUR BODIES ARE VESSELS, WHERE YOUR SPIRIT DWELLS
THE SPIRIT WHICH, I, YOUR LORD, BREATHED INTO YOU
IS ALSO LIGHT, FOR IT IS MY LOVE, WHICH IS TRUE
WHEN AT LAST, MY CHILDREN, I SHALL BRING YOU HOME
WHERE YOU SHALL WORSHIP AROUND THE GREAT THRONE
ETERNAL PEACE SHALL BE YOURS, AND JOY BEYOND MEASURE
WHEN AT LAST YOU BEHOLD, THE MOST HOLY TREASURE

WHEN, I BRING YOU, MY BELOVED, HOME TO ME
YOU SHALL HAVE HAPPINESS, AND YOU SHALL BE FREE
ALL PAIN AND SORROW, SHALL BE WIPED AWAY
WHERE LOVE IS ETERNAL, MY CHILDREN SHALL STAY
FREE, FROM ALL TRIBULATION THAT LIFE CAN BRING
YOU SHALL BEHOLD THE LAMB, YOUR MIGHTY KING
WHO SITS AT THE RIGHT HAND OF THE ALMIGHTY FATHER
HE IS YOUR SAVIOR, YOUR LORD, THE LIFE GIVING WATER
YOU SHALL HAVE KNOWLEDGE YOU HAVE NEVER POSSESSED
WHERE YOU SHALL BE HOLY, AND YOU SHALL BE BLESSED
SINCE YOU, MY CHILDREN, ARE PART OF THE BODY OF CHRIST
SO YOU SHALL SHINE BRILLIANTLY, WITH LOVE'S PURE LIGHT

LET US REJOICE

BROTHERS AND SISTERS, LET US REJOICE, WITH GLADNESS, LET US SING
TO OUR LORD, OUR GOD AND SAVIOR, WHO IS OUR BLESSED KING
HE WHO IS IN THE MIDST OF THE THRONE SHALL SEND UPON US ALL
THE FIRE OF HIS HOLY SPIRIT, SO THAT IN SIN WE MAY NOT FALL
FOR HE IS OUR ALMIGHTY GOD, OUR SALVATION AND OUR SHIELD
TO HIS HOLY WISDOM, AND HOLY LOVE, MAY WE FOREVER YIELD
LET US OPEN OUR HEARTS AND SOULS TO THE HOLY ONE WHO SAVES
FOR HE SHALL PROVIDE ALL THAT WE NEED, IF WE FOLLOW IN HIS WAYS
HE SHARES OUR SORROWS, AND OUR PAIN, HE WILL BRING US THROUGH
AS PROMISED, HE IS WITH US UNTIL THE END IN ALL THAT WE MAY DO;
GIVES US COMFORT WHEN WE HURT, HE HELPS US TO ENDURE
IF WE ASK WITH TRUST AND FAITH, OUR ILLNESS HE SHALL CURE

SO LET US REJOICE, WITH HIGHEST PRAISE, LET OUR VOICES RING
FOR HE IS WORTHY OF ALL PRAISE, OUR FAITHFUL LOVING KING
SING PRAISE TO HIM WHO WAS RAISED UPON THAT LONELY CROSS
SING PRAISE TO HIM WHO CAME TO CLAIM THE LONELY AND THE LOST
SING PRAISE TO HIM WHO WAS RAISED UP AND FOREVER LIVES
WHO EXTENDS HIS HOLY ARMS TO US, ALWAYS READY TO FORGIVE
SING, OH SING CHILDREN OF THE LIGHT, GIVE GLORY UNTO HIM
FOR HE SO LOVED HIS CHILDREN, HE PAID FOR ALL OUR SINS
THERE IS NO SIN UPON HIM, IN HIM, THERE IS NO SHAME
BUT THROUGH HIS HOLY BLESSED LOVE, OUR SAVIOR TOOK THE BLAME
PRAISE BE TO GOD, THE FATHER, PRAISE TO GOD THE SON
PRAISE BE TO HIS HOLY SPIRIT, HOLY POWERFUL ONE

HE IS OUR MIGHTY, AWESOME GOD, JESUS, NAME ABOVE NAMES
PRECIOUS LAMB, WHO DIED FOR US, HE WHO IS WITHOUT STAIN
PROTECTOR OF THE WEAK, HE WHO TURNED THE OTHER CHEEK
WHEN SINNERS, UPON HIM DID SPIT, HE REMAINED SILENT AND MEEK
HE PRAYED FOR HIS TORTURERS, FORGETTING HIS OWN PAIN
PLEADING WITH THE FATHER, TO FORGIVE THEM IN HIS NAME
THEY DID NOT UNDERSTAND, WHEN THEY NAILED HIS FEET AND HANDS
THAT THEY WERE REJECTING THE SAVIOR, SON OF GOD AND MAN
MY SISTERS AND BROTHERS, BEHOLD THE PROMISE MADE OF OLD
THE VERY ONE, THE HOLY LAMB, BY THE PROPHETS FORETOLD
FOREVER LET US REJOICE, AND LIFT OUR HANDS UP HIGH
TO SHOW OUR GOD, HOW MUCH WE LOVE THE ONE WHO, FOR US, DIED

I SHALL NOT TURN AWAY

LISTEN MY CHILDREN, YOUR GOD HAS THIS TO SAY
NO MATTER HOW MANY TIMES YOU FALL, I SHALL NOT TURN AWAY
FOR I PROMISED ON MY NAME, I WOULD PROTECT MY OWN
SO THEY MAY WORSHIP ME AROUND MY HEAVENLY THRONE
FOR I KNOW THE SPIRIT IS WILLING, BUT AT TIMES THE FLESH IS WEAK
LISTEN CAREFULLY, MY CHLDREN, TO THE WORDS I SPEAK
WHEN YOU FALL AWAY FROM GOD, FOR A TIME HE HIDES HIS FACE
BUT SWIFTLY HE RETURNS TO BRING YOU BACK INTO HIS GRACE
ALL WHO HAVE SORROW FOR THEIR SINS, DO PRAY WITH EARNEST TEARS
FOR GOD IS KIND AND MERCIFUL, HE WILL QUELL YOUR FEARS
I, YOUR LORD, HAVE BROUGHT YOU, THROUGH GRIEF, SORROW AND STRIFE
SO ASK FOR MY FORGIVENESS, FOR I AM THE BREAD OF LIFE

CONFESS ME AS YOUR SAVIOR, ASK ME BACK INTO YOUR HEART
FOR I SHALL EVER REIGN THERE, NEVER TO DEPART
MY PEACE I LEAVE UNTO YOU, MY BLESSINGS I FREELY GIVE
FREELY I LOVE, FREELY I SAVE, AND FREELY I FORGIVE
I AM EVER WAITING, FOR MY WAYWARD CHILDREN TO HEED
THE LAWS OF THEIR SAVIOR, WHICH IS SALVATION INDEED
I ASK YOU TO TRUST ME, WITH A FAITHFUL, LOVING SPIRIT
LET THOSE WITH EYES, PERCEIVE, LET THOSE WITH EARS; HEAR IT
THE LORD IS PERFECT AND HOLY AS YOU SHOULD STRIVE TO BE
BUT IF YOU FALL, ON ME YOU SHALL CALL, FOR ONLY, I, CAN SET YOU FREE

COME BACK TO YOUR SAVIOR'S TABLE, WHERE YOU SHALL BE FILLED
WITH THE HOLY LIVING BREAD OF LIFE, WHO DIED ON CALVARY HILL
YOU SHALL HAVE LIVING WATER, YOU SHALL NEVER THIRST AGAIN
YOU SHALL FIND YOUR ONE TRUE GOD, THE GATEWAY; ENTER IN
FOR HE WHO DIED ON CALVARY HILL, PAID FOR THE SINS OF ALL
NOT ONE PENNY SHALL YOU PAY, WHEN THE LORD ANSWERS YOUR CALL
WHEN YOUR EARTHLY DAYS ARE GONE, YOU SHALL COME TO THE HOLY ONE
THE PERFECT LIVING SACRIFICE, LAMB OF GOD, HIS WILL BE DONE
MY ROD AND STAFF SHALL COMFORT, HE WHO FOLLOWS IN MY PATH
THE LOST, I WILL RESCUE; THE FOUND I SHALL BLESS, AND SAVE FROM THE WRATH
AS LONG AS THERE IS LIFE ON EARTH, UNTIL THE FINAL DAY
MY CHILDREN SHALL FIND ME WAITING, I SHALL NOT TURN AWAY

LORD OF ALL CREATION

OH LOVING JESUS, SON OF GOD, CREATOR OF ALL THINGS
HOW MY HEART DELIGHTS IN YOU, HOW MY SPIRIT SINGS
KIND AND GENTLE, JESUS, SO POWERFUL AND STRONG
I LONG TO SING YOUR PRAISES, FOR MY WHOLE LIFELONG,
FOR YOU, MY SAVIOR, HAVE RESCUED ME, TIME AND TIME AGAIN
FROM POVERTY, FROM STRIFE, FROM SORROW AND FROM SIN
LORD, YOU, WHO KNEW MY SORROWS, MY BURDENS AND MY PAIN
WHEN I WAS DOWN, YOU CARRIED ME, TILL I COULD STAND AGAIN
LORD OF ALL CREATION, MAKE ME PURE IN HEART
SO THAT I MAY EVER FOLLOW YOU; FROM YOU, NEVER TO DEPART
YOU CREATED ME TO WORSHIP YOU, MY GOD, I THEE, ADORE
FATHER, SON AND HOLY SPIRIT, YESTERDAY, TODAY AND FOREVERMORE

TREASURES YOU GAVE ME LORD, LITTLE ONES AROUND MY FEET
WHEN I WOULD COME HOME FROM A WORKDAY, I NO LONGER FELT DEFEAT
I STRUGGLED TO DO ALL I COULD TO RAISE THEM IN THE LIGHT
I DID MY BEST WITH WHAT I HAD TO KEEP THEM STRAIGHT AND RIGHT
IT IS SO DELIGHTFUL, TO WATCH A CHILD DEVELOP FROM A BABE
THE WONDER IN THEIR EYES, AS AT THE WORLD THEY GAZE
BABY SMILES AND EYES SO BRIGHT; WHILE MAKING COOING SOUNDS
SURE THEY WERE PEERING AT THE ANGELS, WHO FOREVER HOVER 'ROUND
TO EACH LITTLE SPIRIT, EACH LITTLE BABE, THAT YOU, MY SAVIOR, SEND
YOU GIVE THEIR OWN PROTECTORS, THEIR ANGELS, GUARDIAN
THANK YOU FOR THOSE LITTLE ONES, WITHOUT THEM I'D NOT HAVE SURVIVED
THEY TURNED MY PAIN TO JOY, WHEN I GAZED INTO THEIR INNOCENT EYES

YEARS HAVE PASSED, TIMES HAVE CHANGED, THEY HAVE CHARGES OF THEIR OWN
THEY ARE YOUNG AND DO NOT KNOW THE DANGERS AWAY FROM HOME
PLEASE LORD LET EACH GENERATION,   RETURN TO FOLLOW THEE
SO THAT THEY MAY HAVE HAPPINESS, PEACE AND JOY, AND TRUE FIDELITY
WITH THEIR SAVIOR, WHO IS PATIENT AND KIND, AND AWAITS TO HEAR THEM ASK
YOU TO COME INTO THEIR LIVES; TO RETURN TO YOU AT LAST
SOME WAYWARD GENERATIONS, ARE CAUGHT UP IN THE WORLD,
CHASING FLEETING PLEASURES, SATAN'S FURY IS UNFURLED
FOR HE HAS NOT MUCH TIME TO STEAL IMMORTAL SOULS, AND FEARS IT
RULER OF THIS WORLD, TILL YOU RETURN, TO BAN HIM TO THE FIERY PIT
SATAN WANTS THEM TO FOLLOW HIM, AND RECEIVE DAMNATION'S ROD
THEY DON'T KNOW THE REASON EVIL ABOUNDS; FOR THE WORLD HAS ABANDONED GOD

LORD, MY HOPE OF SALVATION

OH LORD, YOU ARE MY HOPE OF SALVATION, LET MY VOICE EXALT YOUR NAME
FROM ALL EVIL, MAY I FIRMLY ABSTAIN, MAY I HOLD HONESTY HIGHER THAN GAIN
OH LORD IN WHOM I PLACE MY HOPE, LET MY SONGS OF LOVE ARISE
AND MY SAVING GOD, I PRAY THAT YOU WILL ENLIGHTEN MY EYES
DEAR JESUS, REDEEMER, LORD I ASK THAT YOU GIVE EAR TO MY PRAYER
TO KEEP ME, DEAR SAVIOR, IN YOUR DELICATE CARE
FOR YOU ARE MY GOD, MY FORTRESS, MY STRENGTH AND MY ROCK
WHO SHALL DELIVER HIS SERVANT FROM TEMPEST AND SHOCK
IN MY DISTRESS, I SHALL ALWAYS COME TO MY LORD
HE, WHO WITH LOVE AND COMPASSION, ASSISTANCE, SHALL POUR
OH LORD, PERFECT INDEED ARE YOUR HOLY LAWS OF SALVATION
LORD, WITH YOUR HOLY SPIRIT, MAKE ME A NEW CREATION

CLEANSE ME FROM FAULTS THAT MAY CLING WITHIN
LORD, LET THEM NOT CAUSE ME TO FALL INTO SIN
OH LORD, I LISTEN FOR YOUR MOST TENDER VOICE
YOUR WORDS, LORD, SUSTAIN ME, IN THEM I REJOICE
OH LORD, MAY YOUR PEOPLE EVER GIVE GLORY TO THEE
YOU ARE HONOR AND MAJESTY, AND MIGHTY TO SEE
LORD, YOU ARE MY SHEPHERD, WITH YOU I AM FOUND
LOVE, PEACE, JOY, AND HAPPINESS FOREVER ABOUND
LORD, IN YOUR KINDNESS, FEED THOSE WHO ARE YOURS
KEEP ME WITH YOU LORD, NOW AND FOREVERMORE
UNTO YOU, MY LORD, I DO LIFT UP MY SOUL
HELP ME, OH LORD, TO ARRIVE AT MY GOAL

TEACH ME THE RIGHT PATH LORD, SHOW ME THE WAY
FOR YOUR HOLY GUIDANCE, I SHALL WAIT EVERY DAY
JUDGE ME, OH LORD FOR MY WAY I KEEP TRUE
I SHALL NOT TURN AWAY, FOR MY TRUST IS IN YOU
CLEANSE EVERY THOUGHT, THAT MY ABIDES IN MY HEART
SO THAT FROM YOUR SIDE, LORD, I SHALL NOT DEPART
LORD, YOU, BEING MY REFUGE, THEN WHOM, SHOULD I FEAR
FOR WHEN I AM TROUBLED, MY GOD, YOU REMAIN NEAR
I WILL EXTOL YOUR NAME, OH GOD WHO DOES SAVE
YOU, LORD, HAVE RESCUED MY SOUL FROM THE GRAVE
I WILL GIVE THANKS TO THE LORD I ADORE
AND SING OUT YOUR PRAISES, NOW AND EVERMORE

LET US SING, A NEW SONG

SING TO THE LORD WITH WORDS MIGHTY AND TRUE
GIVE TO THE LORD ALL THE GLORY THAT'S DUE
WORSHIP THE LORD IN THE BEAUTY OF PRAISE
MAGNIFY, JESUS, FOR HIS WONDERFUL WAYS
SING TO THE LORD, WITH DANCING AND JOY
PRAISE HIM WITH MUSIC, LET US MAKE A GLAD NOISE
FOR HE SPOKE THE WORD, AND ALL THINGS WERE MADE
THE VERY FOUNDATIONS OF EARTH, HE DID LAY
TASTE NOW AND SEE, HIS GOODNESS AND GRACE
SING OF OUR DESIRE TO BEHOLD HIS DEAR FACE
SING OUT HIS PRAISE, ALL YOU WHO TRUST IN THE LORD
AND HE SHALL SEND, TO YOU, GRACIOUS REWARD

SING TO THE LORD, A NEW SONG FULL OF LOVE
TO THE KING OF THE WORLD, WHO DID ASCEND FROM ABOVE
SING PRAISES FOREVER MAKE HEAVEN YOUR GOAL
FOR HE IS THE KEEPER, OF OUR WAYWARD SOULS
SING OF HIS POWER, AND KINDNESS, FOR HE IS JUST
BLESSED IS HE WHO HOLDS HIM AS HIS TRUST
FOR GOD IS THE DESTROYER OF EVIL AND STRIFE
GOD IS THE GIVER OF HEALTH AND OF LIFE
WHY, WALK IN SADNESS, WHY BE THOU, DOWNTROD
LET US SING PRAISE TO HIM, OUR HOPE AND OUR GOD
HE IS OUR SAVING GOD, LET US EXALT HIM ON HIGH
FOR HIS CREATION, ON THE CROSS, HE DID DIE

LISTEN MY BROTHERS AND SISTERS OF EARTH
AND YOU SHALL HEAR A SAYING OF WORTH
NO ONE, BY RICHES, CAN RANSOM HIS SOUL
WEALTH YOU MAY HAVE, YET WILL DEATH TAKES IT TOLL
LISTEN, THEN AND HEAR THE WORDS OF THE LORD
HE IS THE OWNER OF ALL THINGS OUTPOURED
WASH US OH LORD, AND BLOT OUT ALL OUR SINS
CLEANSE AND RENEW, LORD, OUR SPIRIT WITHIN
LET NOT YOUR SPIRIT, LORD, FROM US DEPART
KEEP US; HOLD US CLOSE TO YOUR SACRED HEART
SO LET US SING TO THE LORD, WITH THANKSGIVING AND PRAISE
FOR IT IS HE WHO SAVES HIS CHILDREN, FROM TROUBLESOME DAYS

LIKE WINGS OF A DOVE

OH THAT I WOULD HAVE THE WINGS OF A DOVE
I WOULD FLY TO THE HEAVENS TO SEEK OUT MY LOVE
FOR THIS WORLD WITH HATRED AND EVIL ABOUNDS
VIOLENCE AND STRIFE, EVERYWHERE TO BE FOUND
MY LOVE, WHO HAS MADE ME, WOULD CALL ME TO HOME
THAT I MAY KNEEL AND WORSHIP HIM AT HIS GREAT THRONE
FOR HE IS MY HELPER, JOY OF MY LIFE, BALM OF MY SOUL
BUT THE ENEMY, IS ON A RAMPAGE, OUR SPIRITS HIS GOAL
FOR MY LOVE, WOULD CONSOLE ME AND DRY ALL MY TEARS
HE WOULD GENTLE MY HEART, AND CALM ALL MY FEARS
OH HOW I LONG TO HEAR, HIS SWEET, GENTLE VOICE
SAYING, COME UNTO ME, HOW I WOULD REJOICE

IN THE SHADE OF HIS WINGS, WOULD MY LOVE BID ME REST
GIVING HIS SERVANT, RETREAT FROM THE TEST
LORD, IN MY FEAR, I WOULD COME UNTO YOU
THEN YOU WOULD DEFEND ME IN ALL THAT I DO
OH LORD REACH DOWN FROM YOUR HEAVENS ON HIGH
ADORN ME WITH WINGS, AND BID ME TO FLY
STRAIGHT TO YOUR SACRED ARMS, I WOULD COME
TO MY LOVE, MY MASTER, MAY THY WILL BE DONE
WHERE I SHALL NOT WITNESS, THE WICKED WHO STRAY
AND I WOULD BEHOLD MY GOD, DAY TO DAY
BUT I MUST BE PATIENT, AND WAIT ON MY LORD
FOR HE SHALL HEAP UPON ME, HEAVENLY REWARD

AT DAWN I SHALL SEEK THEE TO WALK IN THY LIGHT
FOR YOU WILL KEEP ME SAFE THROUGH THE DARK NIGHT
YOU WHO HAVE SET THE MOUNTAIN AND STILLS THE DEEP SEAS
WHO BRINGS US THE RAIN, AND THE COOL SUMMER BREEZE
LORD, GOD, MY LOVE, I SHALL SING THEE MY PRAISE
TO OFFER YOU THANKS FOR YOUR LIFE GIVING WAYS
I SHALL SING SOFTLY, FOR ONLY YOUR EARS
SONGS OF CONTENTMENT, OF LOVE AND GOOD CHEER
FOR YOU ARE MY LOVE, MY GOD, IMPARTER OF GRACE
AND YOU SHALL SHOW ME YOUR MOST HOLY FACE
LET YOUR KIND MERCIES FLOW, WITH YOUR BLESSINGS AND LOVE
AND MY SOUL SHALL TAKE WINGS, LIKE THOSE OF A DOVE

JESUS, IS OUR SHIELD

JESUS IS OUR SHIELD, OUR ROCK, OUR SALVATION
AND HE SHALL RULE OVER EACH AND EVERY NATION
THE LORD, CAME DOWN FROM THE HEAVENS ABOVE
TO SHOW US HIS KIND AND MERCIFUL LOVE
MEEKLY, HE WITHSTOOD, THE FATHER'S CHASTENING HAND
HE WITHOUT SIN, OR BLEMISH, TOOK HIS STAND
FOR HIS SINFUL CHILDREN, WHO WERE IN GREAT STRIFE
HE LOVINGLY, GRACIOUSLY, OFFERED HIS LIFE
FOR IN THE DIVINE PLAN, AS IT WAS FORETOLD AND ORDAINED
A PRECIOUS LAMB OF GOD, WITHOUT BLEMISH OR STAIN
WOULD LIFT HIS CHILDREN FROM THE MIRE AND MUD
AND FOR THEM, HE WOULD PAY WITH HIS OWN PRECIOUS BLOOD

JESUS, OUR ROCK, OUR SALVATION, OUR LORD
THE WORD, QUICK AND POWERFUL, LIKE A DOUBLE EDGED SWORD
HUMBLED HIMSELF, AND LIKE FLINT SET HIS FACE
DETERMINED, TO BRING HIS CHILDREN BACK INTO GOD'S GRACE
BORN IN A MANGER, WRAPPED IN SWADDLING CLOTHES
THE KING SPOKEN OF, BY THE PROPHETS OF OLD
HIS BIRTH BY A VIRGIN, WHO CONCENTED TO BE
THE MOTHER OF GOD, TO SET THE WORLD FREE
SHEPHERDS WHO ABIDED IN THE HILLS WITH THEIR SHEEP
HEARD NEWS FROM HEAVENLY HOSTS, THE PROMISE TO KEEP
FOR OUT OF ZION HILLS, CAME THE SAVIOR, OUR PRECIOUS LORD
WHO WAS BY THREE MYSTERIOUS KINGS, MUCH ADORED

HE GREW AND LEARNED JUST WHAT WAS TO BE
THAT HE WOULD SHED HIS BLOOD FOR YOU AND FOR ME
HE CHOSE THE FOLLOWERS GIVEN TO HIM BY THE FATHER
AND SET OUT TO BE, OUR LIFE GIVING WATER
MANY HEALINGS HE DID PERFORM AND LEFT IN HIS WAKE
FOR HE KNEW THAT THE SOULS OF MANKIND WERE AT STAKE
HE TAUGHT HIS DISCIPLES, JUST WHAT TO DO
TO CARRY ON HIS WORK WITH HIS COVENANT NEW
FOR HE WOULD ARISE FROM THE DEAD IN THREE DAYS
AND SOON WAS CRUCIFIED, AND IN THE TOMB HE DID LAY
AND AS PROMISED, DID RAISE UP AS THEY DID DECLARE
WHEN THEY LOOKED IN THE TOMB, THE MESSIAH WASN'T THERE

MOTHER, NEVER FORGOT

OH LORD, MY GOD, MY SAVIOR, HEAR ME AS I PRAY
MAY I CLING TO YOUR TRUTHS, MAY I WALK IN YOUR WAYS
FOR WITH YOU MY GOD, DOES MERCY ABOUND
MAY YOUR BLESSED NAME, IN PRAISE, ON MY LIPS BE FOUND
LORD, I HAVE CRIED, IN THE DAY AND THE NIGHT
THAT YOU MIGHT RESCUE ME FROM MY TROUBLESOME PLIGHT
HEAL ME OH LORD, HEAR MY PLEAS ON THIS DAY
IN YOUR LOVING MERCY, TAKE MY ILLNESS AWAY
LORD, I GIVE OVER MY LIFE UNTO THEE
TO REIGN OVER ME, IN WHATEVER YOU PLEASE
I MAKE YOU KING OF MY HEART, MY BODY AND SOUL
MAY IT PLEASE THEE, JESUS, TO MAKE ME WHOLE

YOU HAVE BEEN WITH ME LORD, THROUHOUT MY WHOLE LIFE
YOUR EVERLASTING LOVE, HAS BROUGHT ME THROUGH STRIFE
YOU RESCUED ME LORD FROM ABJECT POVERTY
CHILD OF A WIDOW, WITH SEVEN BEFORE ME
STILL, I THANK YOU FOR MY WONDERFUL MOTHER
WHO THROUGH TRIAL AND STRIFE, GAVE LOVE LIKE NO OTHER
SHE CARED FOR ME WITH A MOTHER'S UNSELFISH LOVE, TRUE
WHEN DAD WAS KILLED ON THE JOB, I WAS LESS THAN TWO
SHE TOLD ME ALL ABOUT YOU, PRECIOUS SAVIOR AND KING
WHO DIED FOR US ALL SO THAT YOU MAY BRING
OUR PITIFUL SOULS TO WORHSIP AROUND YOUR GREAT THRONE
MAY I PLEASE SEE HER AGAIN, WHEN YOU CALL ME HOME

LORD, I PRAY ALSO, THAT MY DAD IS WITH YOU
FOR TO HIS MEMORY, MOTHER, WAS ALWAYS SO TRUE
SHE NEVER FORGOT HIM OVER THE LONG YEARS
I REMEMBER, WHEN SHE COULD NO LONGER HIDE HER TEARS
I KNEW NOT WHY SHE CRIED, FROM LOSS OR TASK AHEAD
BUT TO SEE HER WEEP, WAS MY YOUNG HEARTS DREAD
MY LORD, KEEP ME ON THE STRAIGHT PATH TO YOU
SO I CAN SEE MY DAD, TO WHOM MY MOM WAS EVER TRUE
AND IN YOUR ABIDING LOVE, KEEP THE ENEMY FROM ME
AND WHEN MY LIFE IS THROUGH, MAY I ABIDE WITH THEE
TO AT LAST MEET MY DAD, WHO I REMEMBER NOT
TO SEE HIM WITH MY MOTHER, FOR SHE NEVER FORGOT

SING TO YOUR GOD

MY CHILDREN, LET ME HEAR YOUR PRAISES, LET YOUR VOICES RING
I LONG FOR MY CHILDREN, FOR I AM YOUR KING
BECAUSE I AM YOUR SHEPHERD, AND YOU ARE MY FLOCK
YOUR SURE FOUNDATION, YOUR SAVIOR, YOUR ROCK
SING OF MY GLORY, MY WONDER AND MY WORTH
FOR YOU, MY CHILDREN, I DESCENDED TO EARTH
I LEFT MY GLORY, MY POWER AND MY THRONE
TO ASSURE MY CHILDREN A PLACE IN MY HOME
MY HOME WHERE TREASURES AWAIT THOSE WHO OBSERVE
MY PRECEPTS AND TEACHINGS; I AM THE LIVING WORD
FOR GREAT IS YOUR LORD, AND HOLY IS HIS NAME
HIS HONOR AND MAJESTY, YOU MUST PROCLAIM

FOR I HAVE MY MIGHT AND MY MAJESTY PROVED
MY COVENANT ESTABLISHED WHICH CANNOT BE MOVED
LET THOSE WITHIN HEARING, HEAR, LET THOSE WITH EYES SEE
WHAT IS IT THAT YOU NEED, THAT YOU HAVE NOT RECEIVED
GOD HAS, BY ME, HIS GRACIOUS SALVATION, MADE KNOWN
ALSO HIS RIGHTEOUSNESS, HAS BEEN FREELY SHOWN
MAKE A LOUD NOISE, REJOICE AND SING PRAISE
FOR GOD HAS REMEMBERED HIS MERCIFUL WAYS
LET THERE BE JOY, AND LOUD EXALTATION
FOR JESUS IS KING OVER ALL THE EARTH'S NATIONS
THE SPIRIT IS MOVING, GOD'S WILL TO BE DONE
HOLY THE FATHER, HOLY THE SPIRIT, HOLY THE SON

COME MY CHILDREN, SING; CLAP YOUR HANDS
FOR AGAINST THE ENEMY, YOUR LORD SHALL MAKE A STAND
YOU WHO BEHAVE IN THE WAYS THAT ARE RIGHT
I SHALL NOT FORSAKE, NOR CAST FROM MY SIGHT
HE WHO HAS EVIL IN HIS MIND MUST DEPART
YE THAT ARE FAITHFUL, SHALL DWELL NEAR MY HEART
BLESS NOW YOUR LORD, WHO CLEANSES YOUR SOULS
WITH HIS OWN SWEET BLOOD, AS PROMISED OF OLD
FOR HE LOOKS ON YOUR HEARTS, AND NOT ON YOUR SIN
HE WHO HAS USHERED, SWEET REDEMPTION IN
GIVE UNTO THE LORD, THAT WHICH IS HIS DUE
FOR HE IS THE ONE, WHO HAS RESCUED YOU

MANY YEARS AGO

LONG AGO AND FAR AWAY, A GREAT STAR APPEARED,
PEOPLE BEHELD IT FROM FAR AND FROM NEAR
LEADING TO THE PLACE, WHERE THERE WAS GREAT FEAR
EVIL WAS THE KING WHO REIGNED ON THE THRONE; THERE
ENVY AND GREED LURKED IN HIS FOUL MIND, HE WAS EVIL TO THE BONE
IF THEIR WAS A WAY, THE CHILD, HE WOULD SLAY; GOD'S OWN
HE DID NOT WANT TO BOW DOWN, TO THE TRUE KING TO COME
HIS EVIL HEART WAS CONNIVING TO DESTROY THE HOLY ONE
MEANWHILE, IN A LITTLE TOWN OF BETHLEHEM
A VIRGIN, MILD, BROUGHT FORTH HER CHILD, FORETOLD BY ANCIENT MEN
BEHOLD, FROM DARKNESS, THERE CAME A GREAT LIGHT
TRUE SON OF GOD AND MAN, THE FATHER'S DELIGHT

ANGELS SANG TO THE SHEPHERD'S ABOUT THE HOLY CHILD
AND SO THEY WENT TO FIND HIM, AND HIS VIRGIN MOTHER MILD
THREE GREAT KINGS DID FOLLOW, WITH GOLD FRANKINCENSE AND MIRRH
FOLLOWING THE SPECIAL STAR, THAT SHOWED THEM WHERE THEY WERE
JOSEPH STALWARTLY KNELT BY, ADORING THE HOLY CHILD
MARY WAS HIS WIFE, MOTHER OF GOD, SO MEEK AND MILD
WHEN HEROD MET THE THREE KINGS, HE PRODDED THEM IN DECEIT
WHEN YOU FIND THIS NEW KING, TELL ME WHERE; I WILL BOW AT HIS FEET
BUT LEARNING OF HIS TREACHERY, THE KINGS TRAVELLED BY ANOTHER ROUTE
FOR AN ANGEL WARNED THEM, SO THEY KNEW WHAT HE WAS ABOUT
WHEN HEROD LEARNED THAT THEY HAD GONE, HIS FURY WAS DEEP
HE ORDERED THE MURDER, OF BABY BOYS, HE TRIED, THE LAND, TO SWEEP

IN A DREAM WAS JOSEPH WARNED, HE AND MARY AND THE BABE ESCAPED
THEY FLED TO THE LAND TO EGYPT, THE HOLY CHILD, TO KEEP SAFE
THEN, WHEN THEY WERE TOLD THAT HEROD WAS DEAD, SO THEY COULD RETURN
THEY SETTLED IN A TOWN CALLED NAZARETH, A SIMPLE LIVING TO EARN
JOSEPH WAS A CARPENTER, AND SO HE TAUGHT HIS SON
FOR HE MUST GROW TO MANHOOD, THIS HOLY PRECIOUS ONE
HE OBEYED HIS PARENTS AND LEARNED EAGERLY KNOWING WHAT HE MUST DO
THEN, WHEN HE WAS READY, HE CALLED HIS TWELVE, WHICH WERE VERY FEW
PERFORMING MIRACLES, TEACHING IN PARABLES, AND SO GREW HIS FAME
TEACHING LOVE, TEACHING PEACE AND HEALING IN HIS OWN NAME
WHEN THE TIME WAS FULFILLED, THEY RAISED OUR LORD ON HIGH
ON THE THIRD DAY, THEY CAME TO FIND THAT THE LORD DID GLORIOUSLY RISE

GOD WAS NOT THERE

I LOOKED IN THE TAVERNS, THE DARK DUNGEONS OF LIFE
I LOOKED ROUND THE STREETS SO POLLUTED WITH STRIFE
I LOOKED UP IN THE HILLS AND IN VALLEYS BELOW
BUT I COULD NOT FIND HIM, OH WHERE DID HE GO
I LOOKED IN THE SCHOOLS, THE LIBRARIES, THE STORES
I LOOKED ROUND THE CITIES AND DOWN BY THE SHORE
I LOOKED IN THE CHURCHES, THE HOUSE OF HIS NAME
BUT STILL I COULD NOT FIND THE SAVIOR WHO CAME
IN THE DARK ALLIES, I SAW OUTRAGEOUS SINS
I TURNED AWAY QUICKLY, FOR GOD WAS NOT IN
I LOOKED OVER EARTH, AND UP IN THE AIR
I LOOKED TO THE PEOPLE, BUT GOD WAS NOT THERE

OH CHILDREN, OH CHILDREN, WHAT FOLLY THIS BE
HAVE YOU CAST OUT OUR GOD, WHO HAS SET YOU FREE
I KEEP LOOKING AND LOOKING AND SEE ONLY BLANK STARES
I LOOKED IN THEIR EYES, BUT MY GOD WASN'T THERE
FOR THE WORLD HAS TURNED AWAY FROM OUR SAVING GOD
WITH DRUGS, AND FORNICATION, AND NO CARE FOR HIS LAWS
FINALLY, I LOOKED IN THE GREAT FIELDS OF GRAIN
I FIND SOME OF HIS FOLLOWERS, OH PRAISE JESUS'S NAME
THEY ARE TRYING TO CONVINCE PEOPLE TO RETURN TO GOD
TO REPENT AND BE SAVED, FROM THE PUNISHING ROD
I LOOKED IN MY HEART AND I FOUND MY GOD THERE
WE FEW MUST CONTINUE, TO SHOW THAT WE CARE

FOR EVIL SATAN, HAS ROAMED THIS DARK WORLD
WITH SO LITTLE TIME, HIS WRATH IS UNFURLED
HE TOLD THEM THAT THEY SHOULD NOT PRAY IN THE SCHOOLS
AND THOSE WHO SANG ANTHEMS TO GOD WERE JUST FOOLS
THEY TOOK GOD FROM THE CHILDREN, AND THREW HIM AWAY
FOR UNBELIEVERS COMPLAINED THAT THEIR CHILD HAD TO PRAY
TURN BACK, TURN BACK, I CRY, TURN BACK TO THE LORD
FOR WITH OUR GREAT GOD, IS MERCY OUTPOURED
OH LORD, HELP YOUR CHILDREN, TO SHOW THEM THE LIGHT
HELP US TO SAVE THEM, FROM THE DARKEST NIGHT
LORD, CHANGE ALL THEIR HEARTS FROM THE OLD TO THE YOUTH
LET THEM KNOW THAT YOU ARE THEIR SURE HOPE, ABIDING IN TRUTH

CROWN OF GLORY

JESUS, MOST HOLY LAMB OF GOD, LIVING SACRIFICIAL LAMB
WE GIVE YOU ALL PRAISE AND HONOR AS WE LIFT OUR HEARTS AND HANDS
YOU WHO NOW REIGN OVER ALL, FOR ALL HAS BEEN GIVEN UNTO YOU
WITH GLAD REFRAIN, WE WORSHIP YOU, OUR GOD, IN SPIRIT AND IN TRUTH
WE THANK YOU LORD, FOR ALL YOU DO FOR YOUR CHILDREN EVERY DAY
YOU ARE THE KING OF GLORY, FOR YOUR CHILDREN, YOU LIGHT THE WAY
WE PRAISE YOUR NAME, THE ONE WHO CAME, TO SAVE US, WHO WERE LOST
THE PRICE IS PAID, OUR SOULS ARE SAVED, FOR YOU DIED UPON THE CROSS
OH HOLY ONE OF ISRAEL, WE PAY HOMAGE TO YOU, OUR KING
YOU WEAR THE CROWN OF GLORY, ADORNED WITH JEWELS OF PRAISES WE SING
AS WE SING WITH JOYFUL HEARTS, THE MUSIC SWIRLS AROUND
EACH SONG OF PRAISE ARE GEMS AND JEWELS FOR YOUR GLORIOUS CROWN

OUR PRAISES RISE UP TO HEAVEN, TO REACH THEE AT THY GREAT THRONE
FOR YOU OUR GOD, HAVE PAID THE COST TO BRING YOUR CHILDREN HOME
AND AS WE SING AND MELODY RINGS, BEAUTIFUL SAVIOR YOU ARE NEAR
FOR YOU INHABIT THE PRAISES OF YOUR PEOPLE, AND YOU ARE REALLY HERE
THE LOVE YOU SHOW FOR YOUR FAITHFUL CHILDREN, IS FAR BEYOND COMPARE
FOR WHEN WE NEED YOU, GLORIOUS LORD, YOU ARE ALWAYS THERE
YOU BRING US GIFTS OF HEALING, OF BODY, MIND AND SOUL
YOU GIVE US GRACE, FORGIVENESS AND LOVE TO MAKE US WHOLE
OH LORD WE PRAY, THAT YOU MAY STAY WITH YOUR SPIRIT SO DIVINE
FOR YOU HAVE SAID, "MY CHILDREN, I LOVE YOU, YOU ARE MINE"
I CLOSE MY EYES AND I SEE RAYS SHINE FROM THY CROWN OF GOLD
EVERY RAY IS A SONG OF PRAISE, SUNG BY THE YOUNG AND THE OLD

THE MORE THE PRAISE, THE MORE THE RAYS, SO DAZZLING AND BEAUTIFUL
WITH COLORS NEVER BEFORE SEEN BY MAN OR EVEN ANGELS
I'VE HEARD IT SAID, OR SOMEWHERE READ PRAYERS ARE SOMEWHAT THE SAME
AS THEY RISE UP TOWARDS YOUR HEAVENLY THRONE, THEY ARE LIKE TINY FLAMES
LORD WE KNOW THAT YOU, OUR GOD ARE THE ONE TRUE HOLY LIGHT
THE SECOND WE BEHOLD YOUR BEAUTY, OUR SOULS WILL THEN TAKE FLIGHT
THE BRIGHTEST LIGHT EMINATES FROM YOU, BRILLIANT YET RESTFUL TOO
FOR YOU ARE, AFTER ALL, PUREST LOVE, WHICH IS LIGHT THAT COMES FROM YOU
AND LORD WE BELIEVE THAT YOU ARE THE ONE TRUE GOD OF MAN
AND WITHOUT YOUR HOLY SPIRIT, LORD, NOT ONE OF US COULD STAND
I READ YOUR WORD AND I AM FED WITH EACH AND EVERY STORY
MAY IT PLEASE THEE BLESSED LORD TO ADORN MY SOUL IN A "CROWN OF GLORY"

WE ARE YOUR CHILDREN

LORD, HOW MAGNIFICENT ARE YOUR TRUTHS, HOW POWERFUL, YOUR LOVE
FROM AGE TO AGE YOU HAVE GIVEN MANKIND CHOICE BLESSINGS FROM ABOVE
WITHOUT YOUR MIGHTY, HOLY LOVE, WHERE WOULD MANKIND BE
WITHOUT YOUR SACRED LOVING HEART, HOW WE WOULD YEARN FOR THEE
YOU ARE PATIENT, KIND AND MERCIFUL, LOVING, LIVING WORD SO TRUE
YOUR GIFTS TO US ARE SO BOUNTIFUL, LORD, ALL WE NEED IS YOU,
WE ARE YOUR CHILDREN, LORD, BECAUSE YOU HAVE CREATED MAN
YOU HAVE GRACIOUSLY WRITTEN OUR NAMES, ON THE PALM OF YOUR HAND
YOU HAVE GIVEN US ENDLESS LOVE, YOU SEND YOUR HOLY SPIRT
YOU GAVE YOUR ONLY SON, WITH WHOM WE SHALL INHEIRIT
JESUS IS OUR SAVIOR, HEAVENLY FATHER, WE THANK THEE
YOU SENT YOUR ONLY BEGOTTEN SON, WHO CAME TO SET US FREE

WE SHALL SING PRAISES TO YOU, DEAR LORD IF IT BE THY WILL
FOR YOU CAME TO EARTH, TOOK ON OUR FLESH, AND DIED ON CALVARY HILL
YET, YOU, LORD, ARE PERFECT AND HOLY IN THE FATHER'S SIGHT
YOU BORE THE SHAME FOR OUR SINFUL SOULS; SAVED US FROM THE DARKEST NIGHT
THERE IS NO LOVE SUCH AS THIS, NOWHERE COULD WE FIND
A LOVE SO POWERFUL AND SO PURE, FOR CHILDREN WHO WERE BLIND
BLIND TO THE TRUTH OF OUR SAVING GOD, WHO CAME AND RANSOMED US
DEAF TO THY GENTLE CALL, BUT NOW WE KNOW, AND IN YOU, WE TRUST
LORD TEACH US TO ALWAYS PUT THEE FIRST AND TO OBEY THY LOVING COMMANDS
WE ARE POWERLESS WITHOUT YOU LORD, WITHOUT YOUR SPIRIT WE COULD NOT STAND
HOW DESOLATE OUR SOULS BECOME WHEN YOU ARE NOT BY OUR SIDE
HELP US ALWAYS TO KEEP YOU NEAR; IN OUR HEARTS MAY YOU RESIDE

MOST BEAUTIFUL GOD OF LOVE AND LIGHT, KEEP US FOREVER TRUE
CREATE IN US, A CLEAN PURE HEART, THAT HAS FIRST PLACE RESERVED FOR YOU
LET US NEVER THINK WE HAVE ENOUGH OF YOU, FILL US WITH YOUR HOLY SPIRIT
LET US BOAST OF OUR LOVING GOD, LET US TAKE OUR FAITH AND SHARE IT
LET US WAKE UP EACH DAY, WITH YOU, THE HOLY ONE, ON OUR MINDS
LET YOUR NAME BE ON OUR LIPS, AND IN OUR HEARTS, FOR ALL TIME
MAY WE EVER THIRST, DEAR LORD, FOR MORE AND MORE OF YOU
NEVER LET US SLEEP AT NIGHT TILL, WE CONVERSE WITH OUR GOD SO TRUE
FOR LORD, IF WE HAVE YOU IN OUR HEARTS, THERE IS NOTHING THAT WE NEED
YOU SHALL CARE FOR US AS YOUR CHILDREN, FOR YOU ARE OUR FATHER INDEED
SINCE WE ARE YOUR CHILDREN LORD, PRAY HELP US REACH OUR GOALS
OH MOST HOLY BLESSED TRINTY, WHO TENDS OUR VERY SOULS

AMEN